CYCLOPED
By Markus Baker

Published by R-and-Q.com.
Copyright © 2018 Mark 'Markus' Baker and R-and-Q.com

All rights reserved.

ISBN: 978-0-9933275-6-8

Please note:

This book's purpose is to share creative skills, interesting stories and imagine what people may look like if they had the 'Cycloped' eye reduction surgery. It also goes on to guess what requirements 'Cycloped' people may have.

The Si Klopp clinic, procedures, surgeons and examples do not exist in the real world. They are all part of a fictional story which is shared in this book and on the accompanying website.

WELCOME

In this book, you will see the work of the world's best fictional cosmetic surgeons and discover the inspiration that led them to develop their patented 'Cycloped' Eye Reduction Surgery.

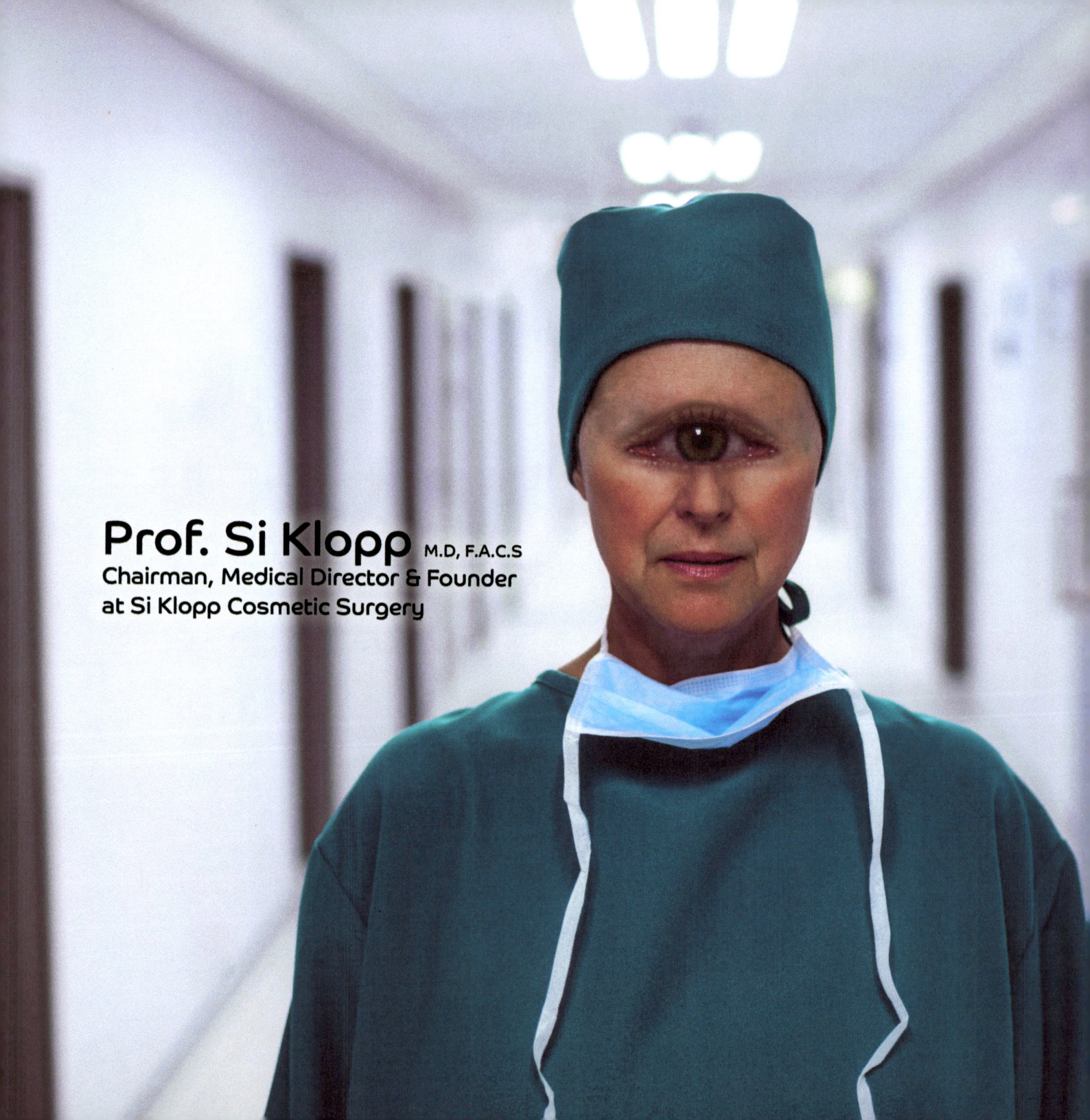

Prof. Si Klopp M.D, F.A.C.S
Chairman, Medical Director & Founder
at Si Klopp Cosmetic Surgery

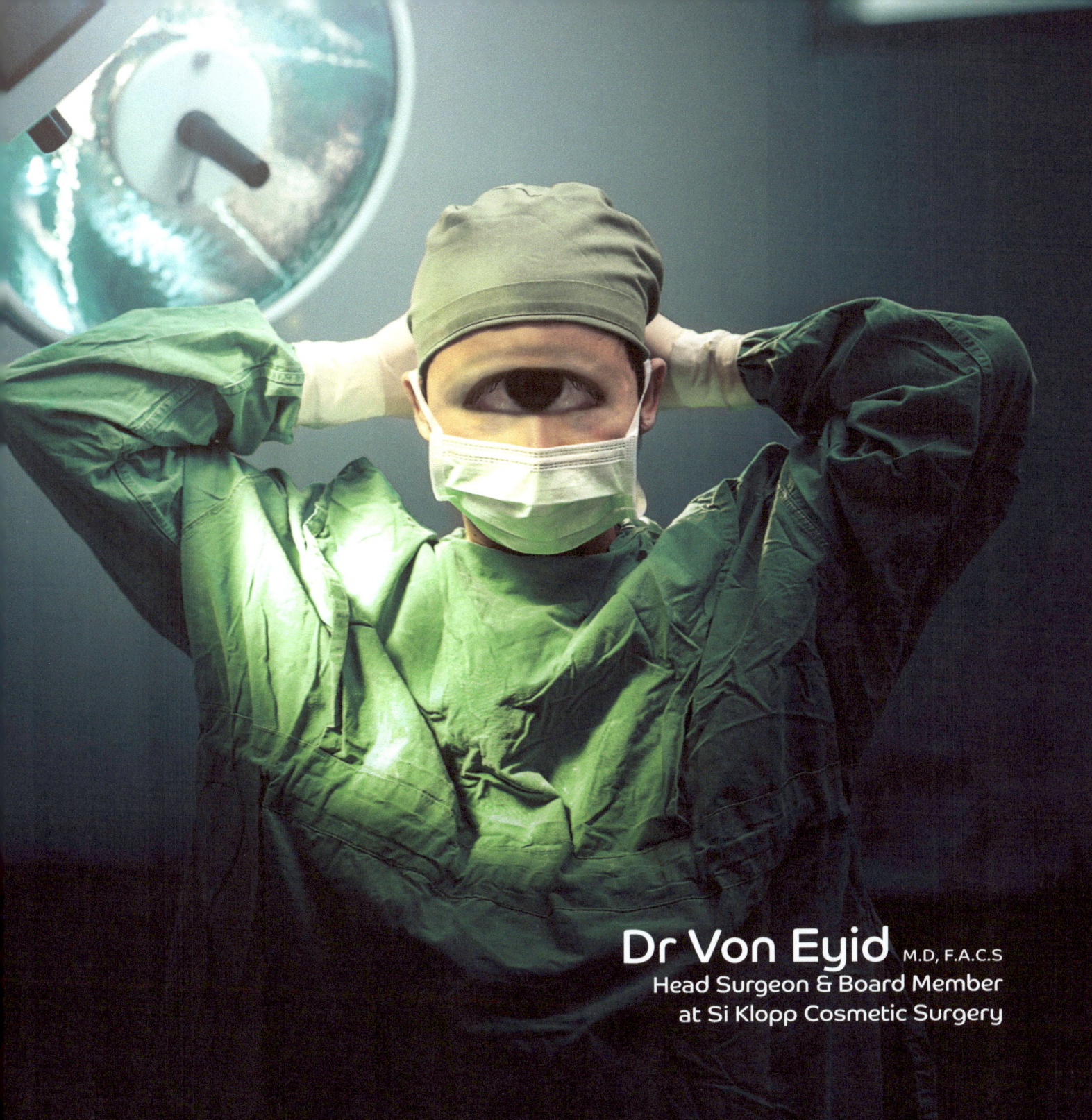

Dr Von Eyid M.D, F.A.C.S
Head Surgeon & Board Member
at Si Klopp Cosmetic Surgery

Introducing the work of the world's most popular cosmetic clinic:

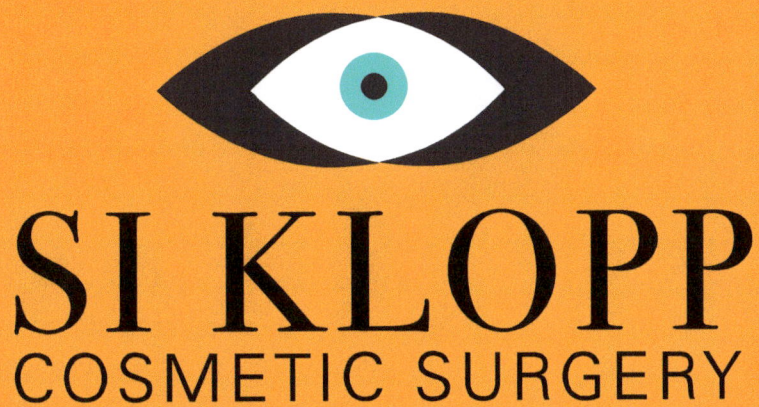

SI KLOPP
COSMETIC SURGERY

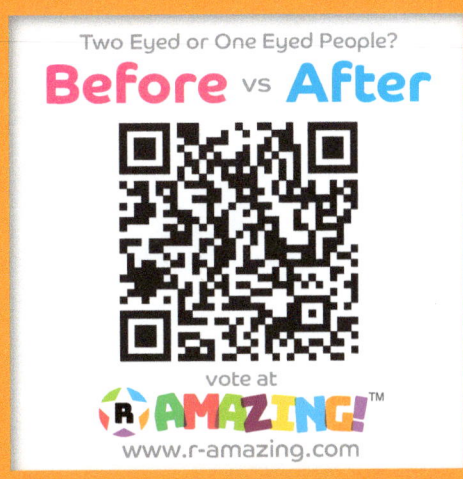

THE CYCLOPED PROCEDURE

1 Professionally and delicately each eye is removed from the face.

2 One eye is safely stored whilst the other is soaked in our patented 'Cycloped' fluid to enable the eye to expand in size.

3 With the perfect mix of strength, gentleness and art we resculpt the face.

4 The resized eye is reconnected with precision and tested to ensure optimal vision.

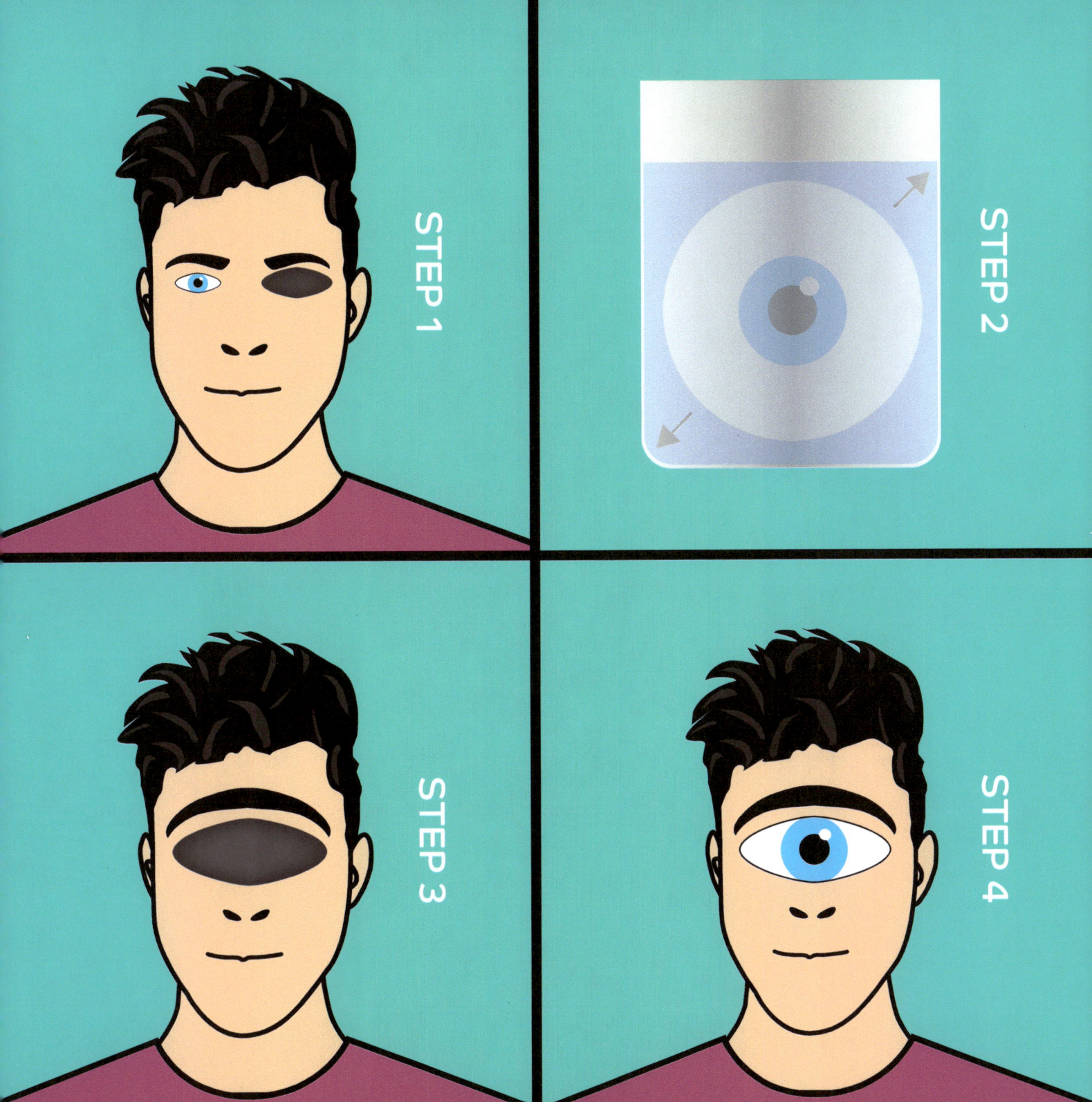

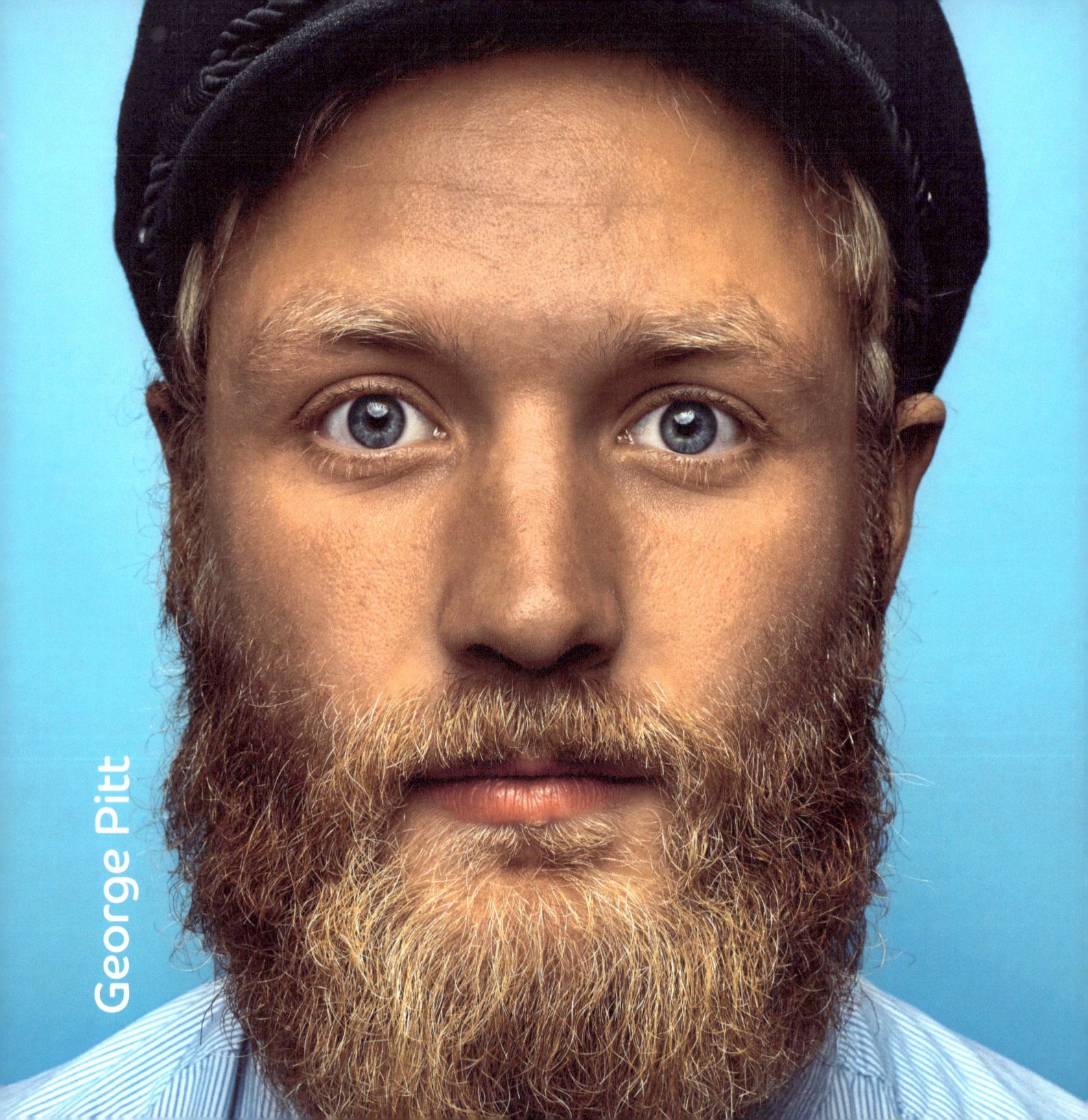

George Pitt

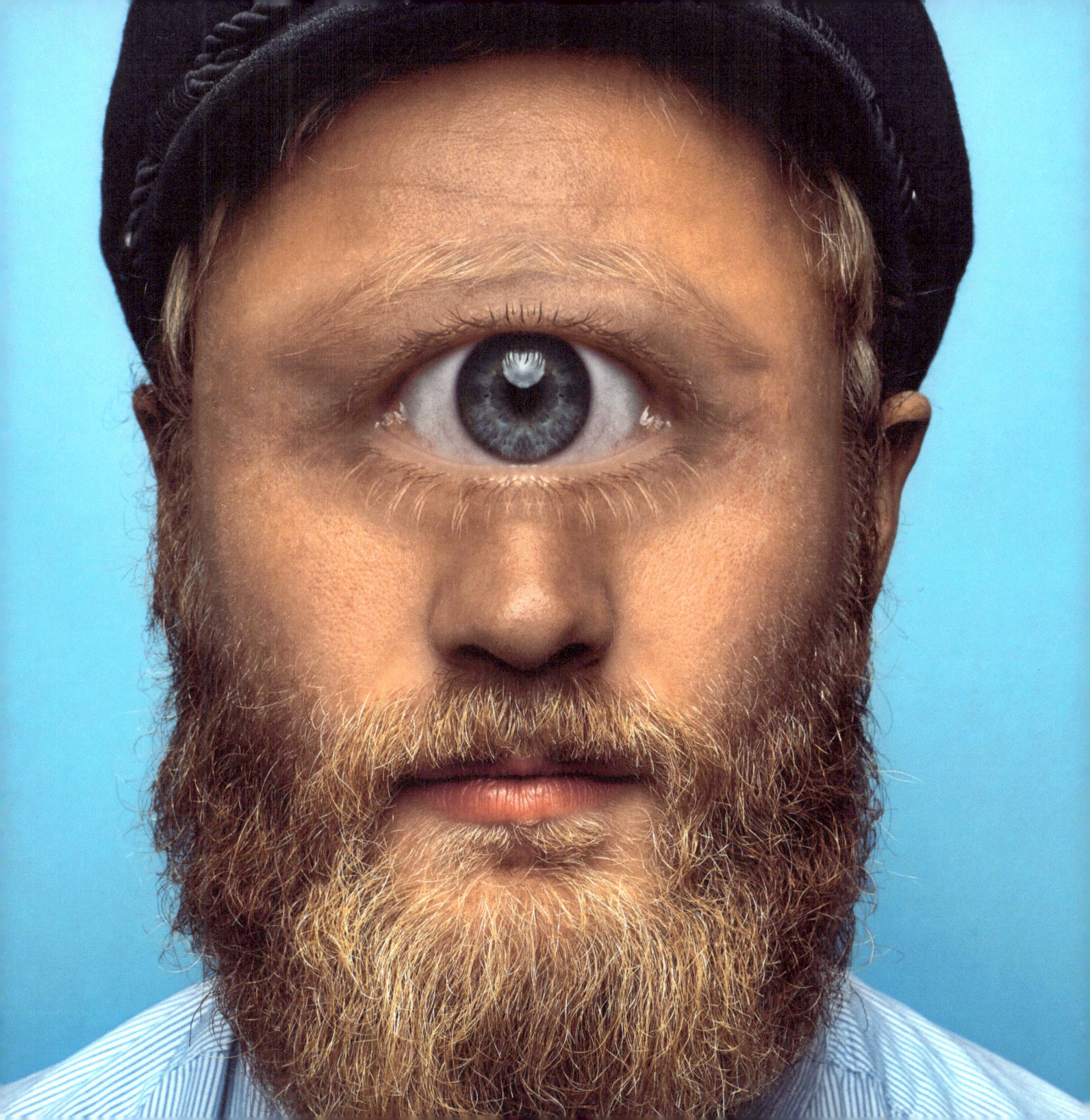

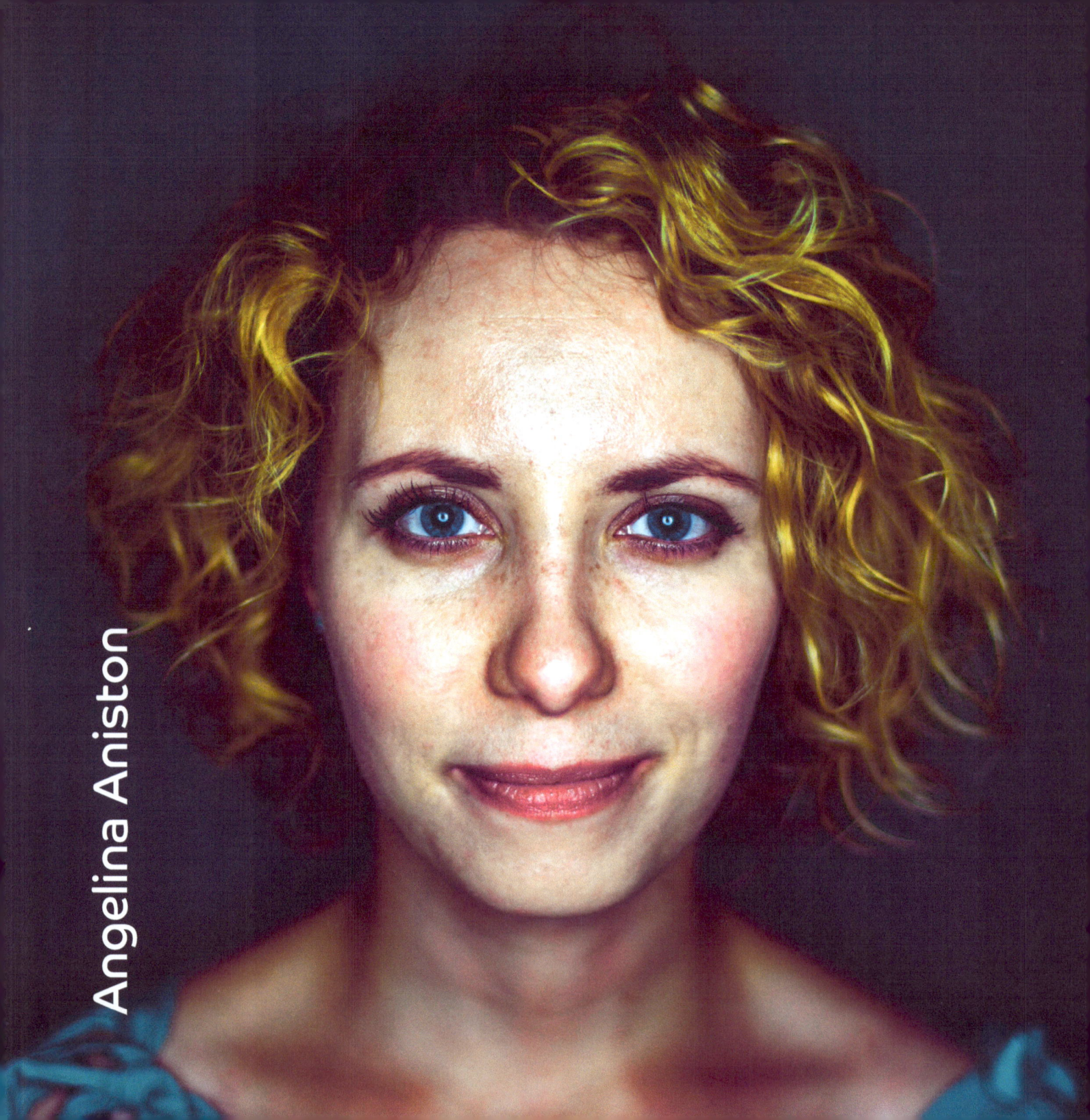

Angelina Aniston

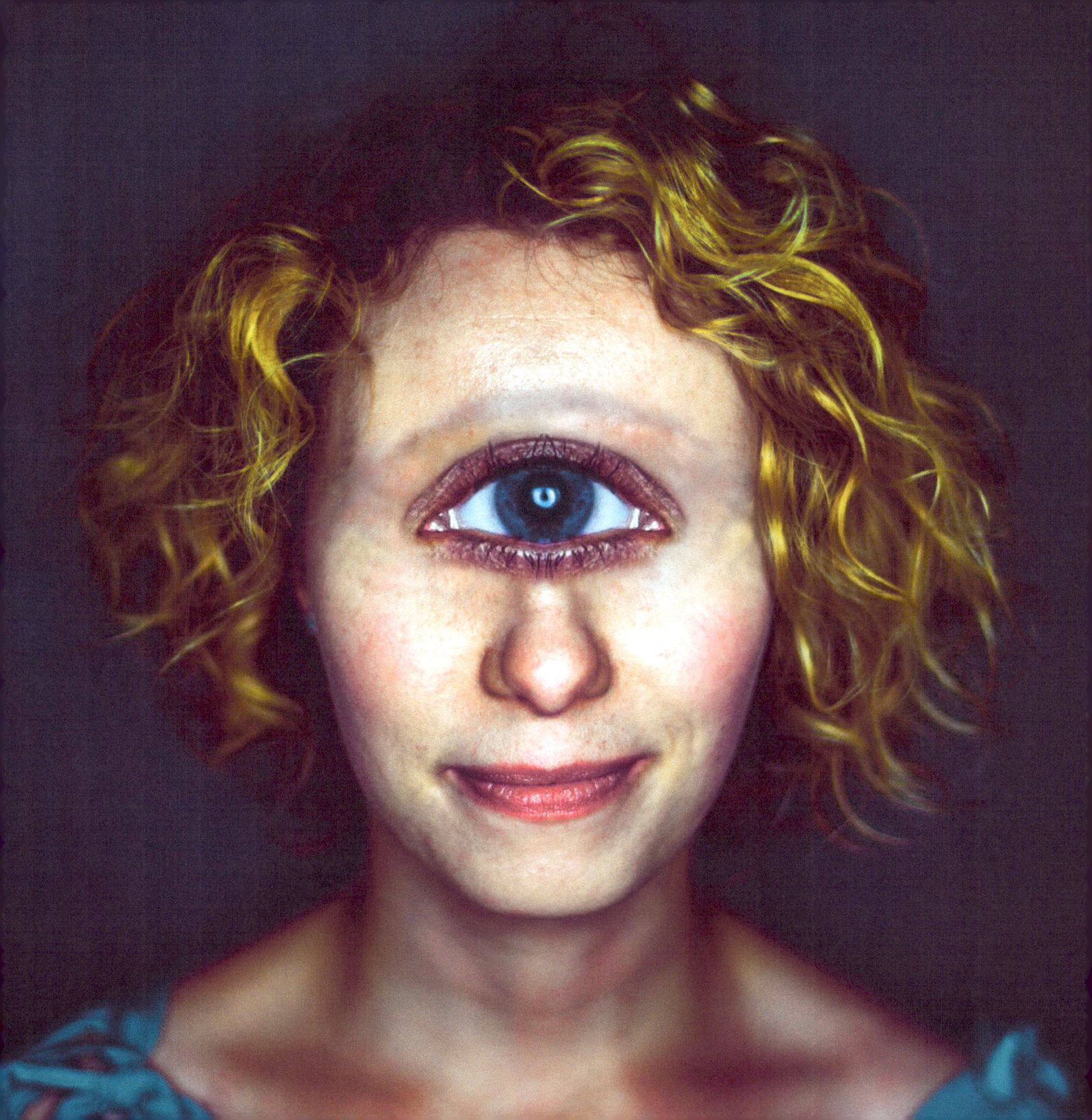

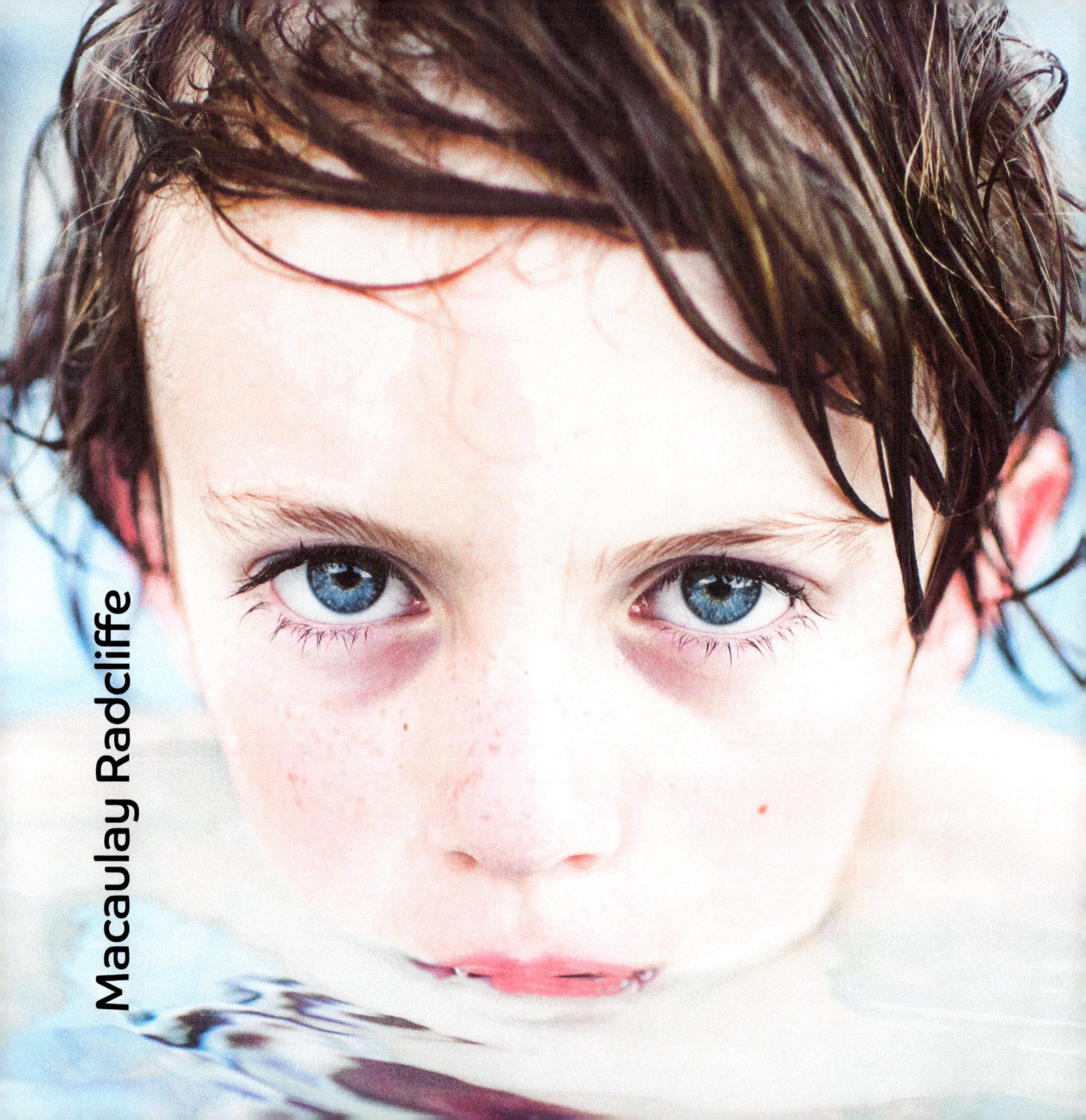

Macaulay Radcliffe

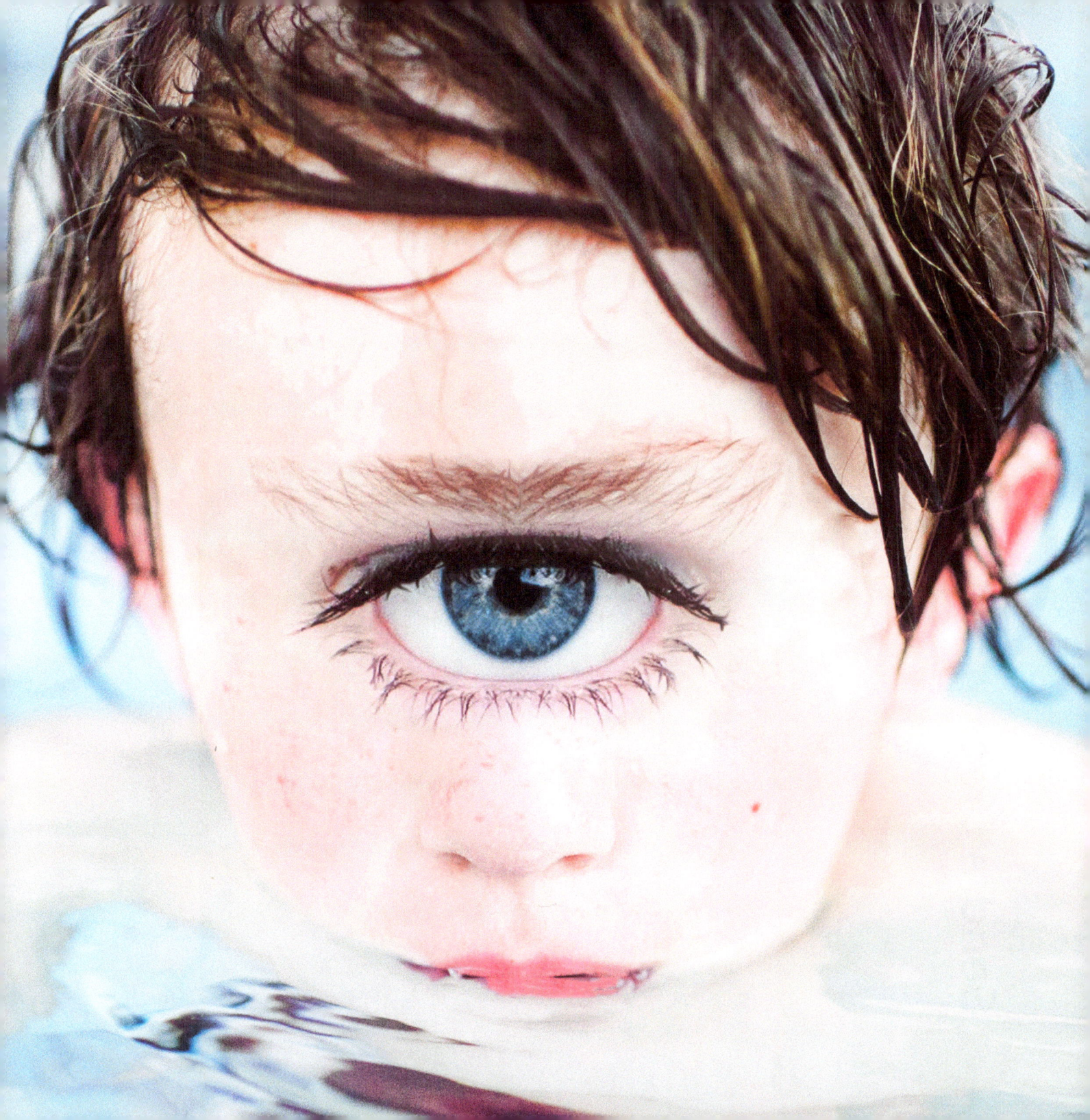

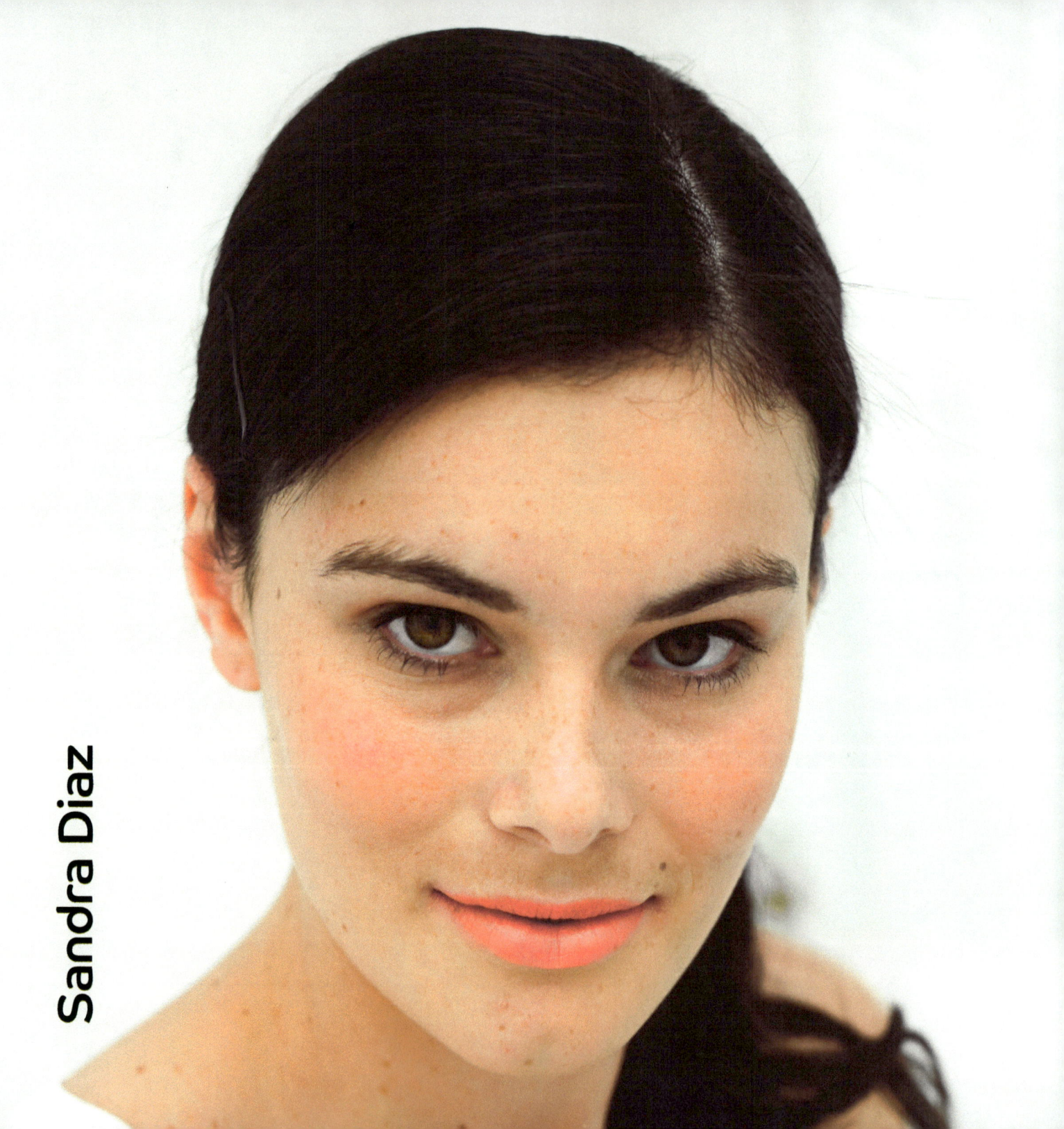

Sandra Diaz

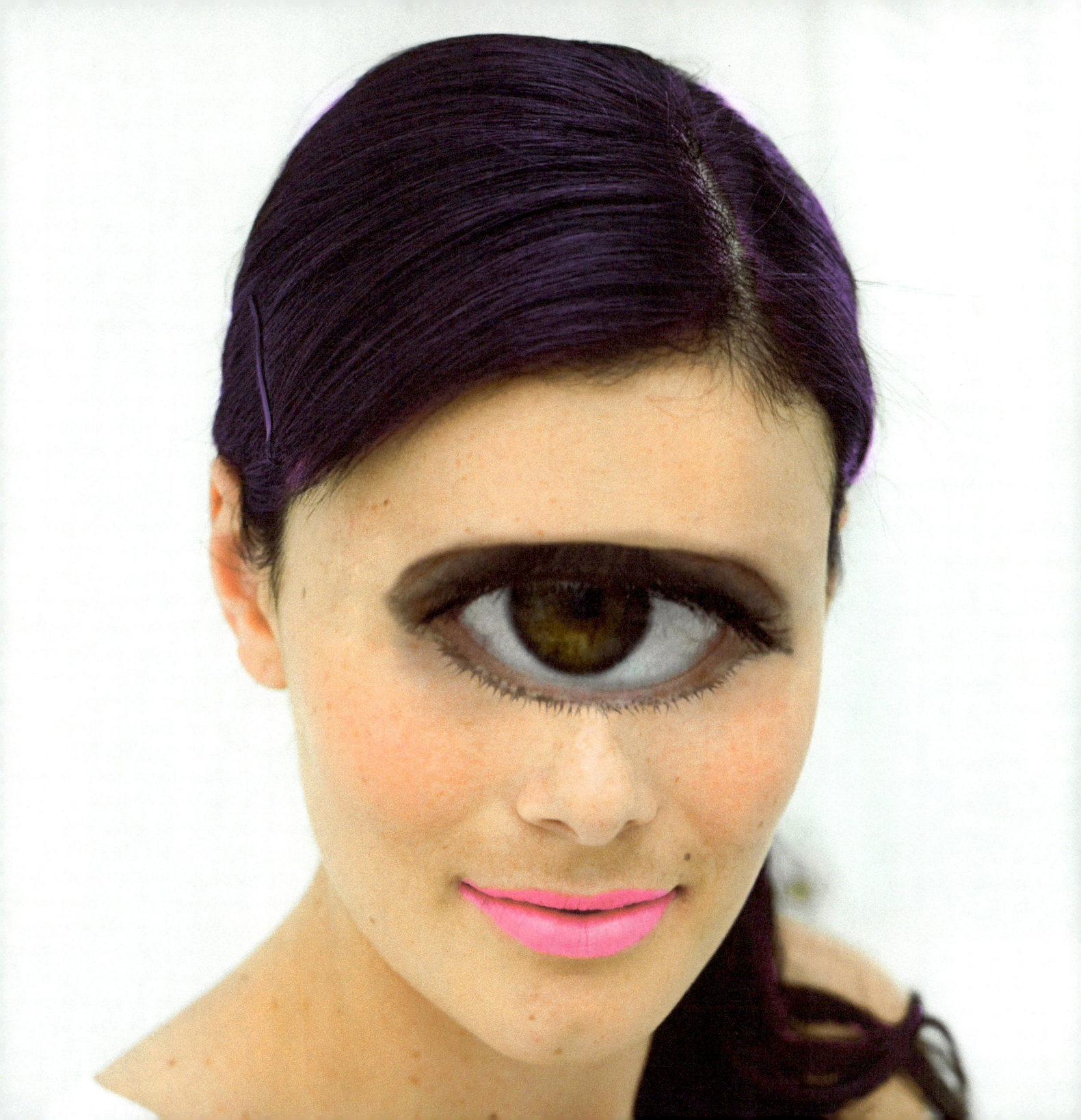

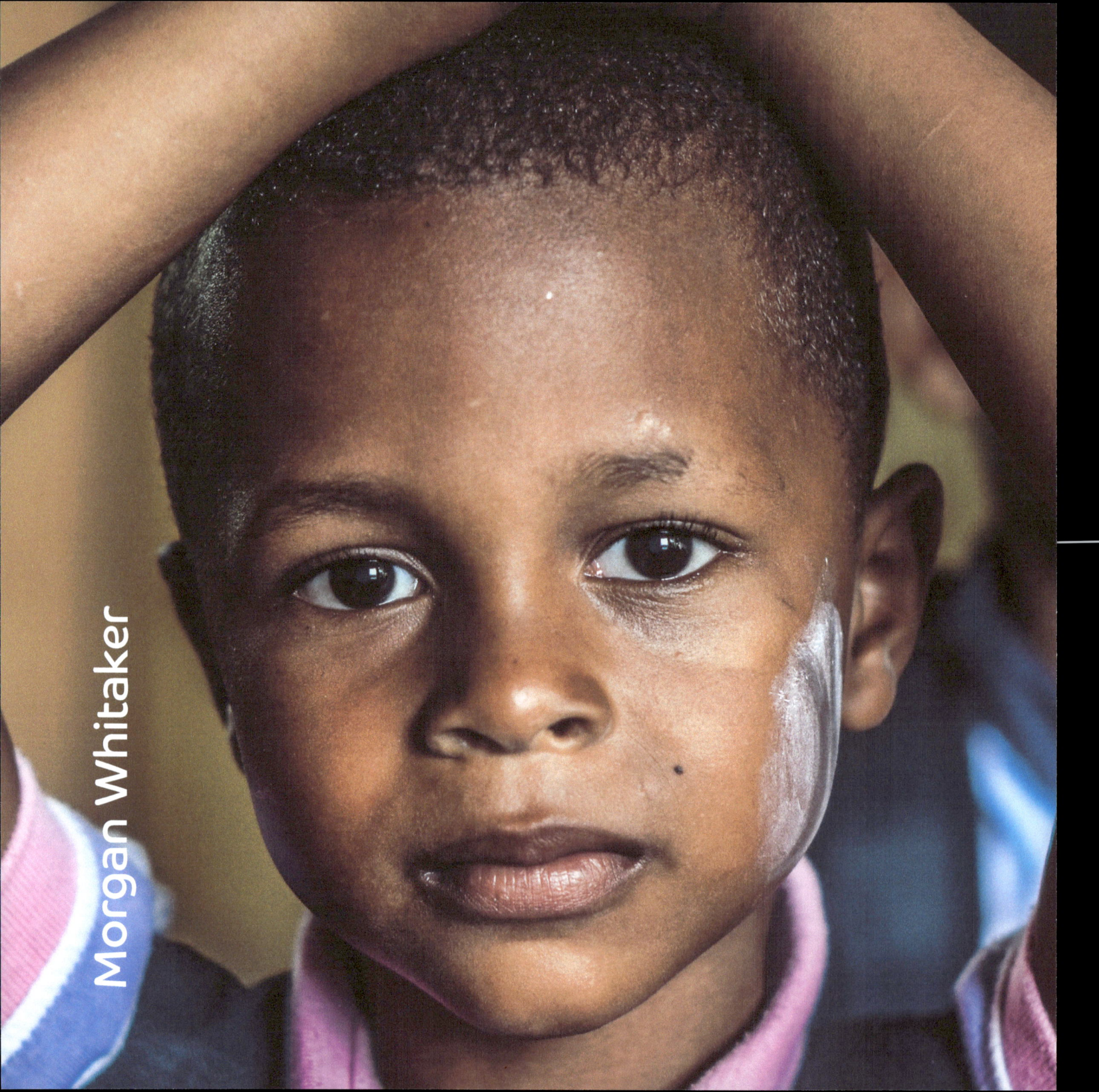

Morgan Whitaker

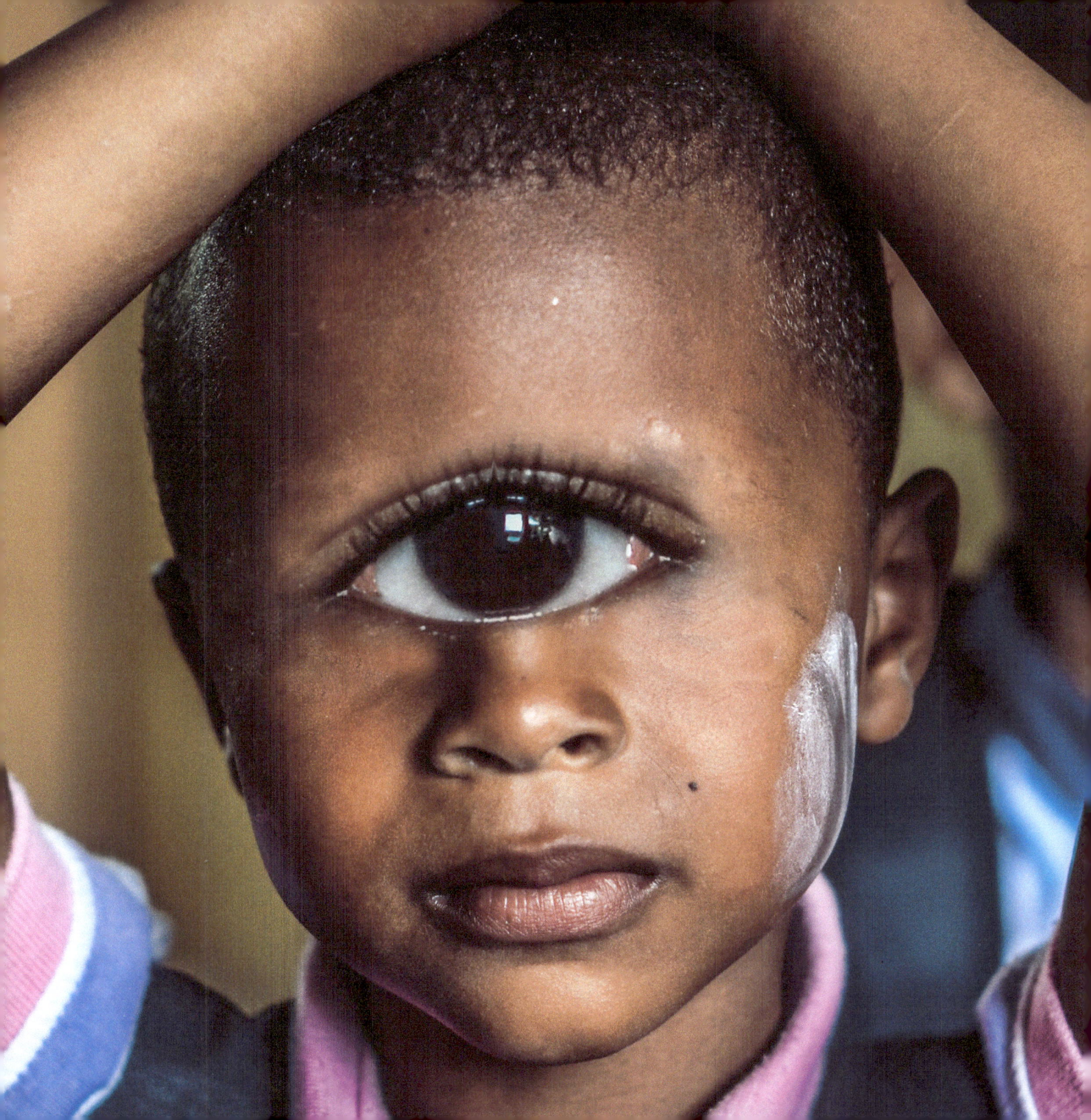

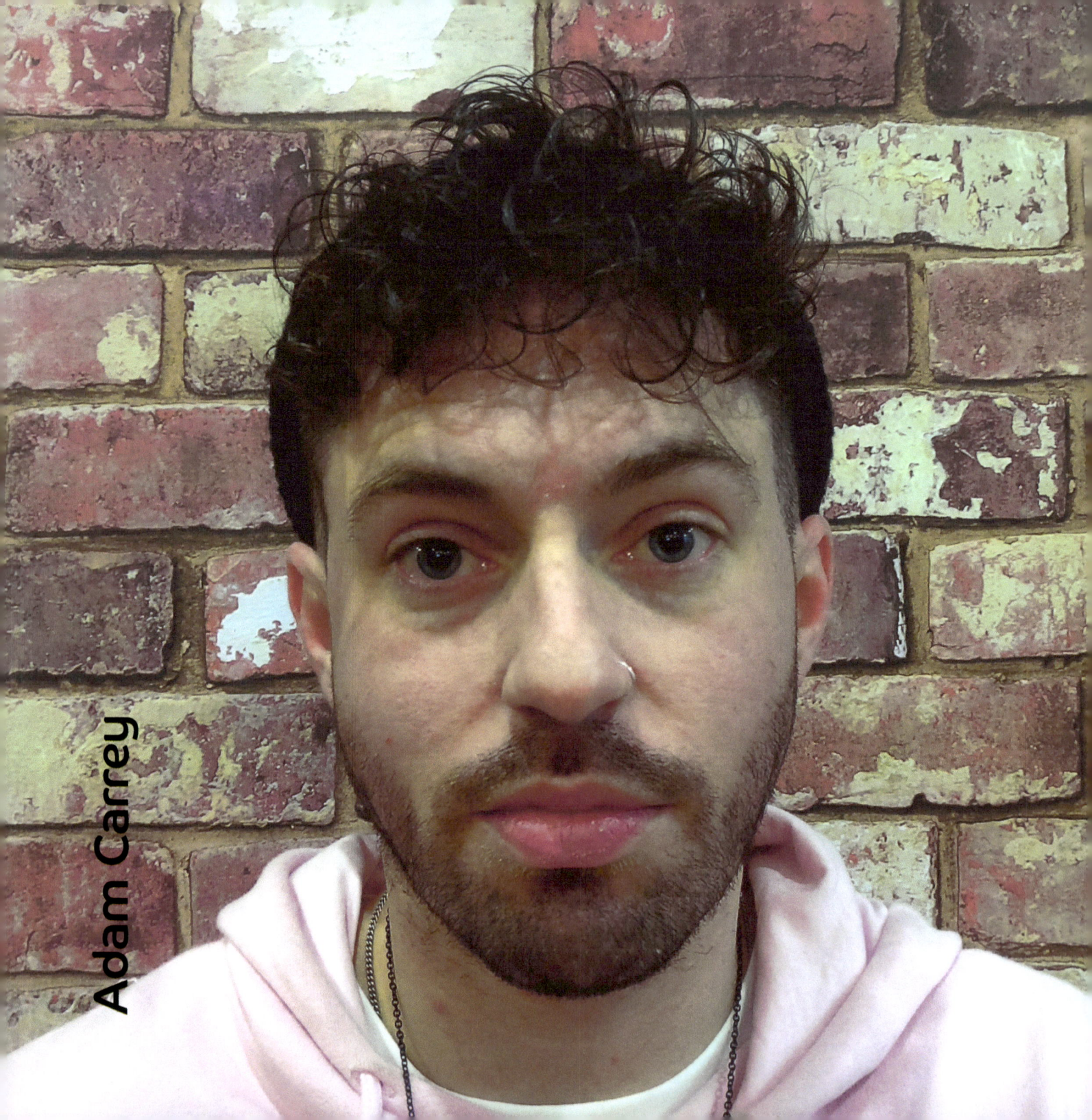

Adam Carrey

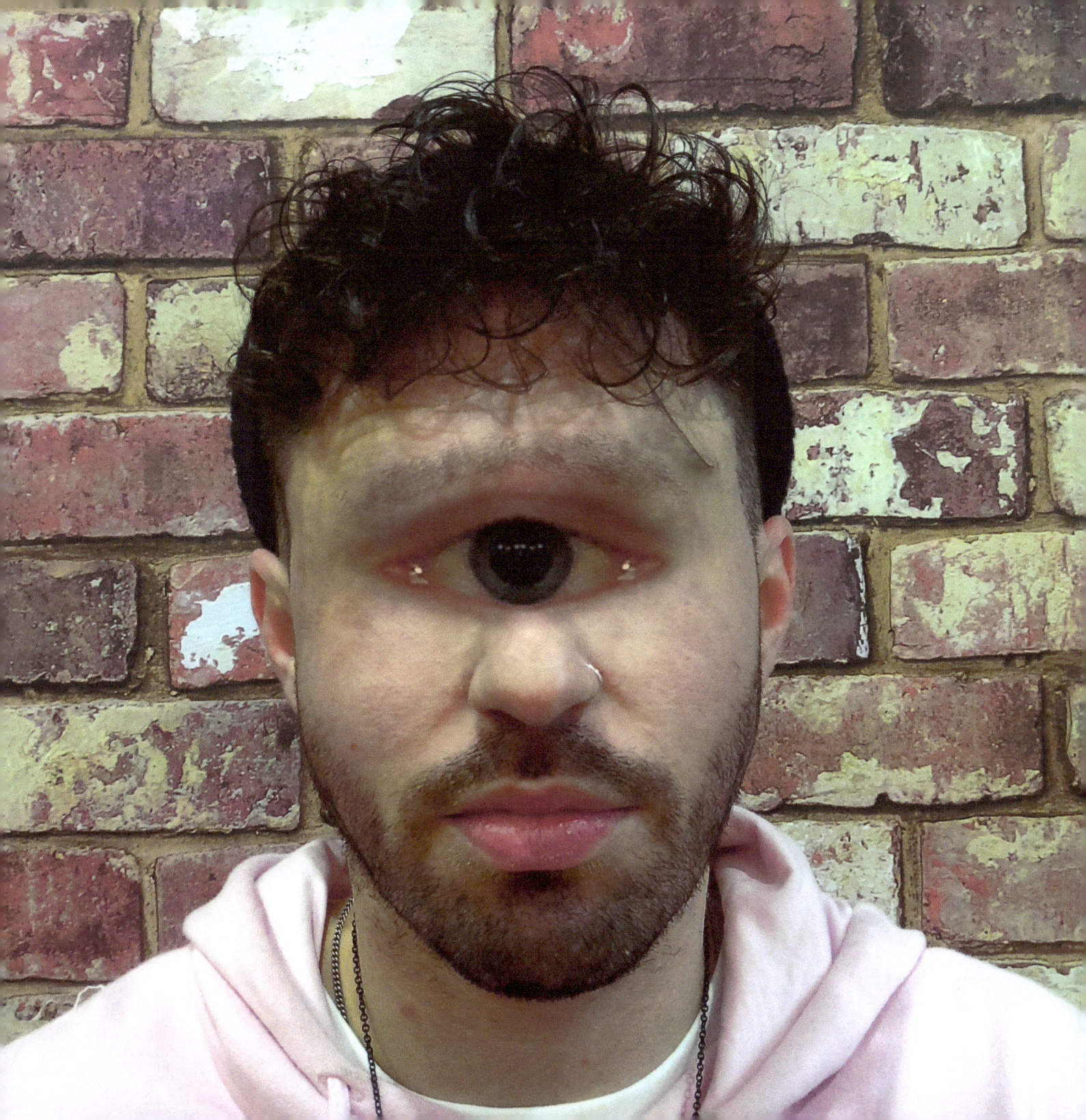

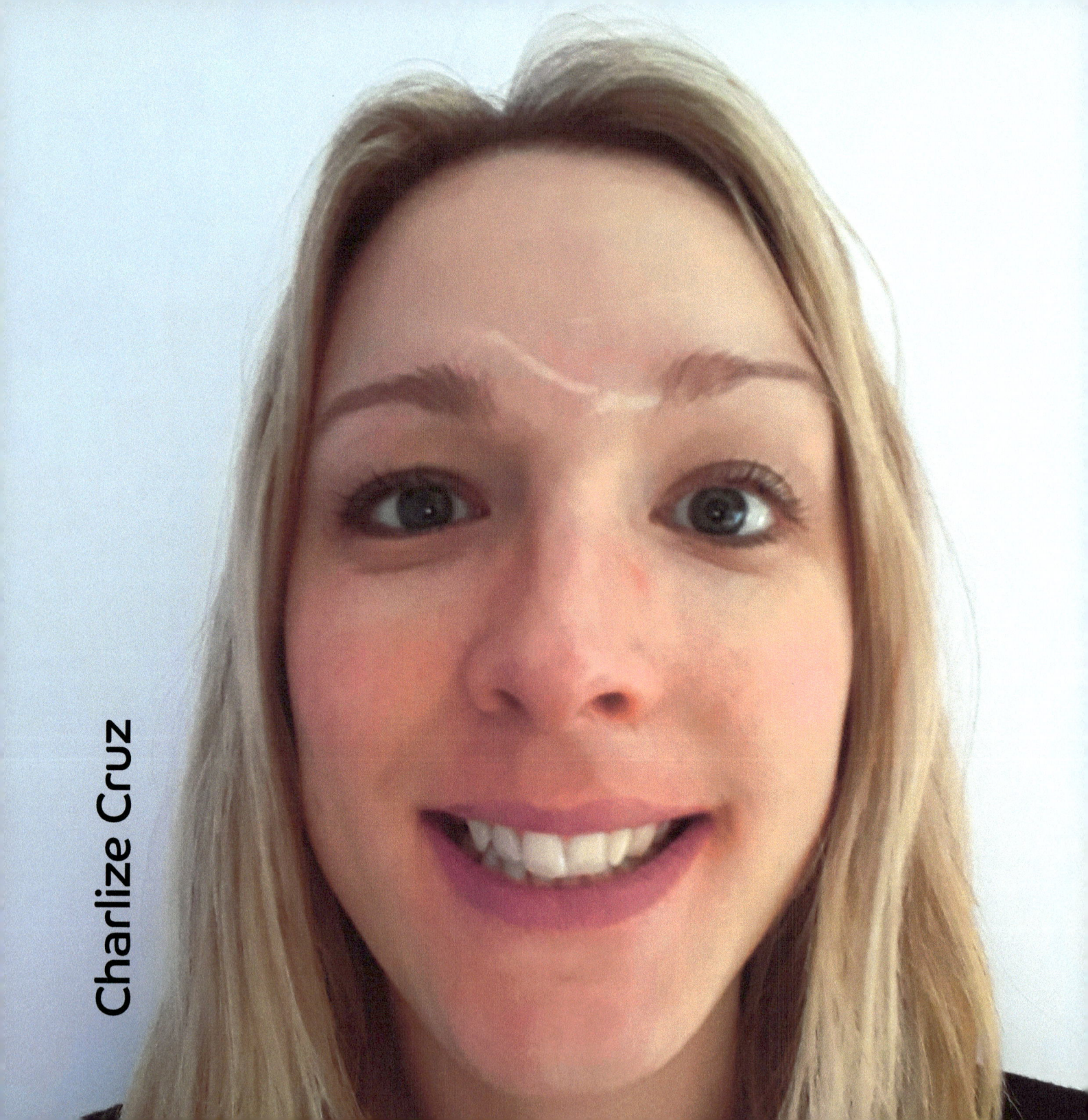

Charlize Cruz

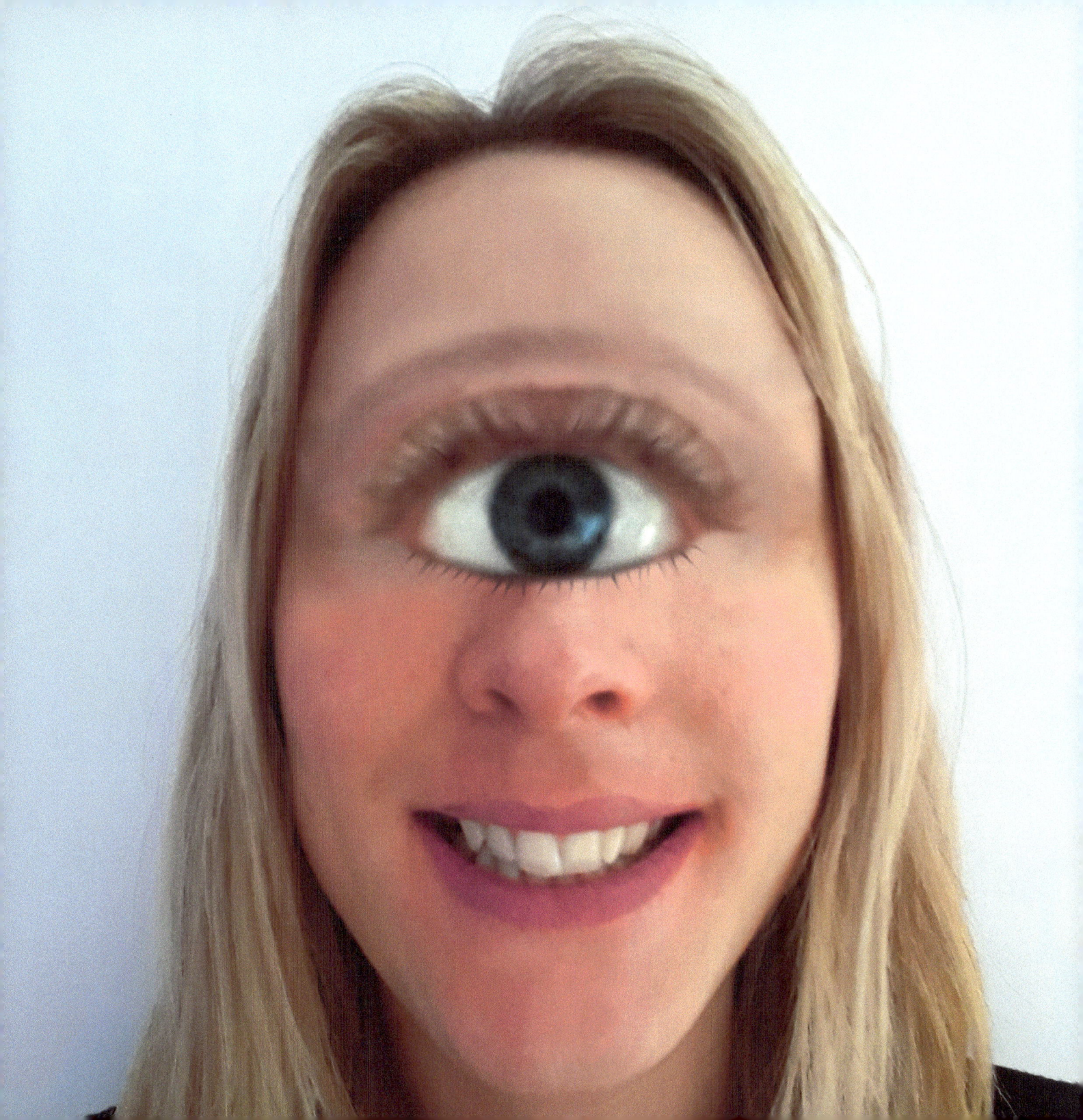

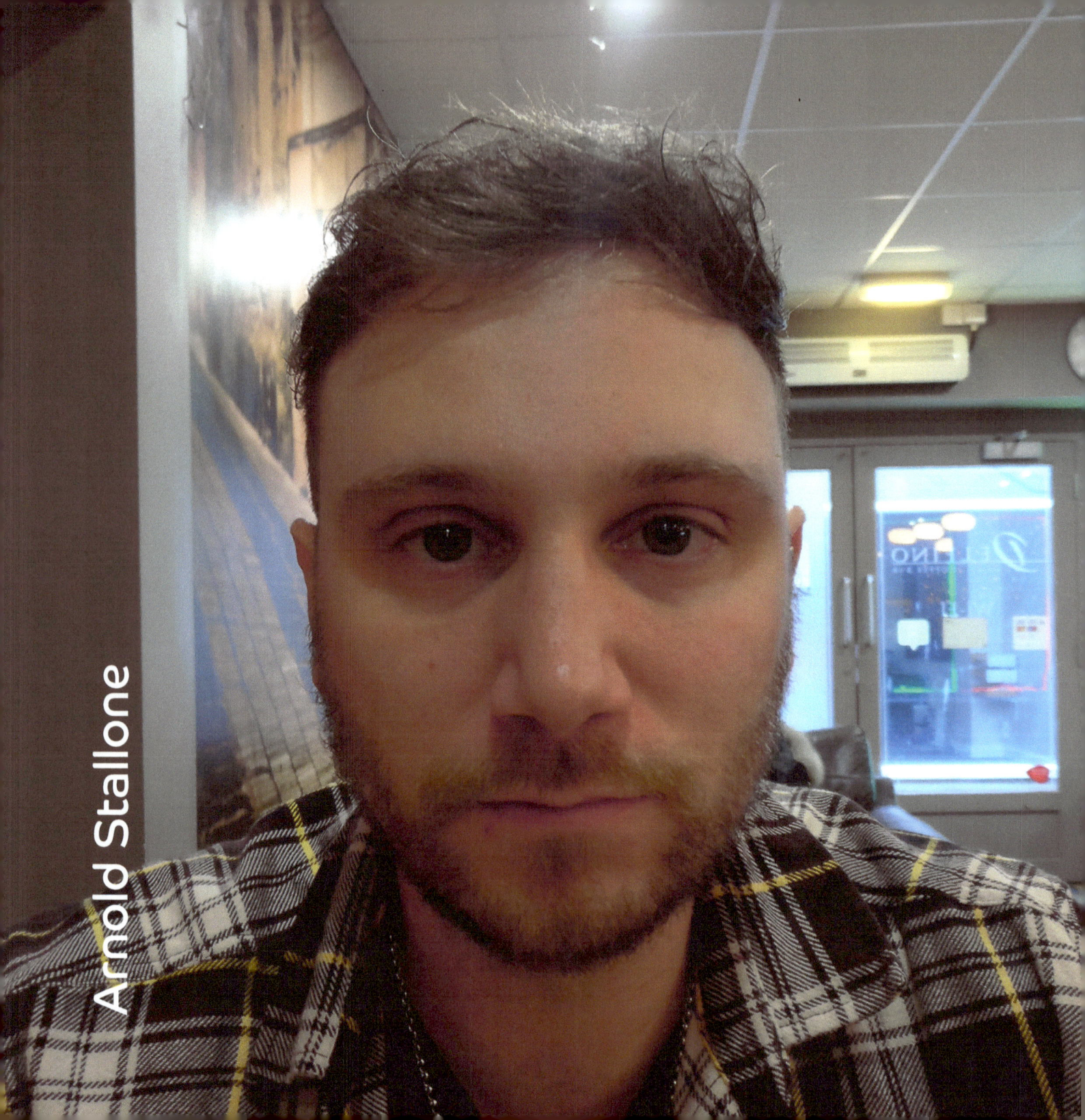

Arnold Stallone

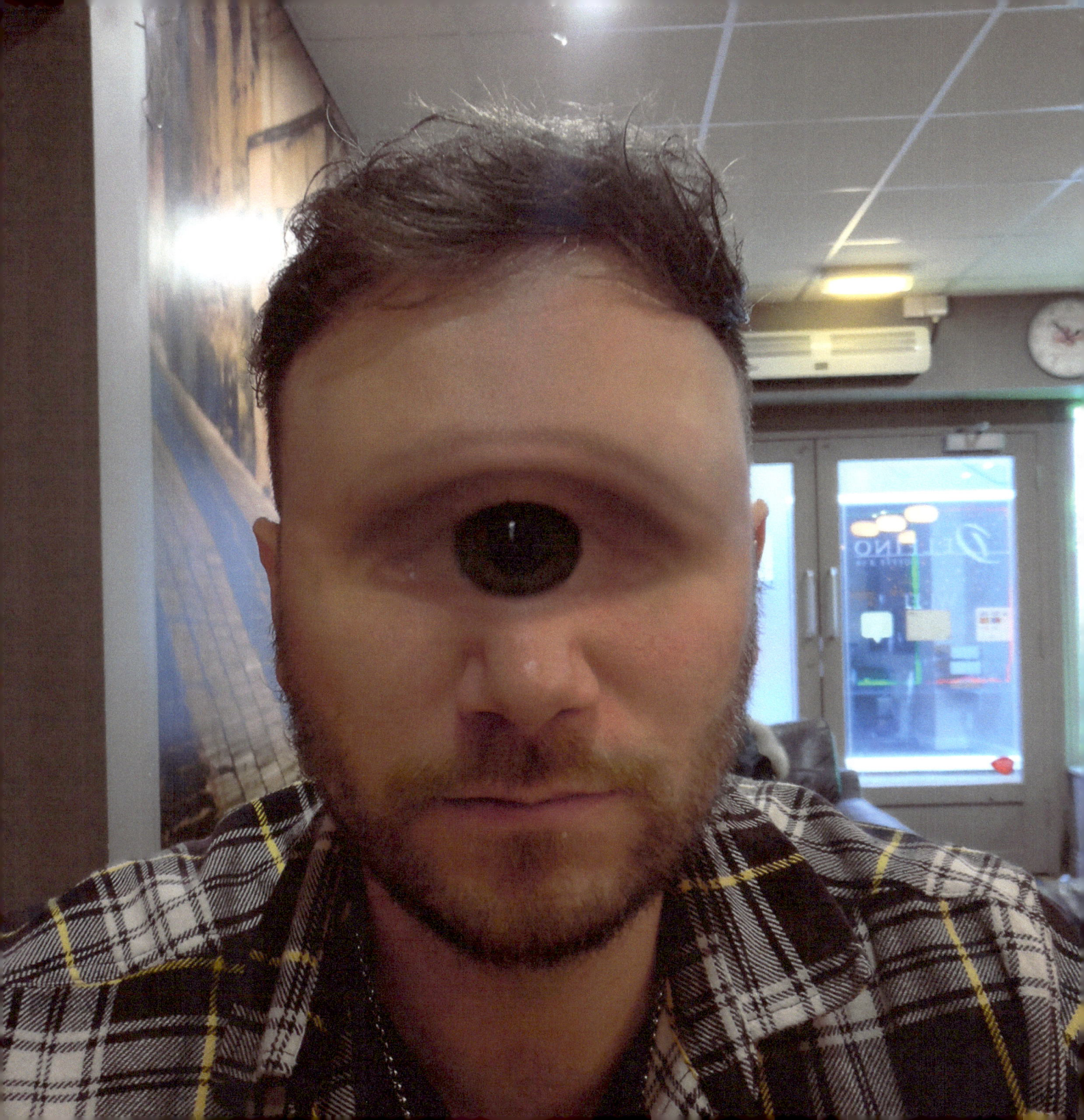

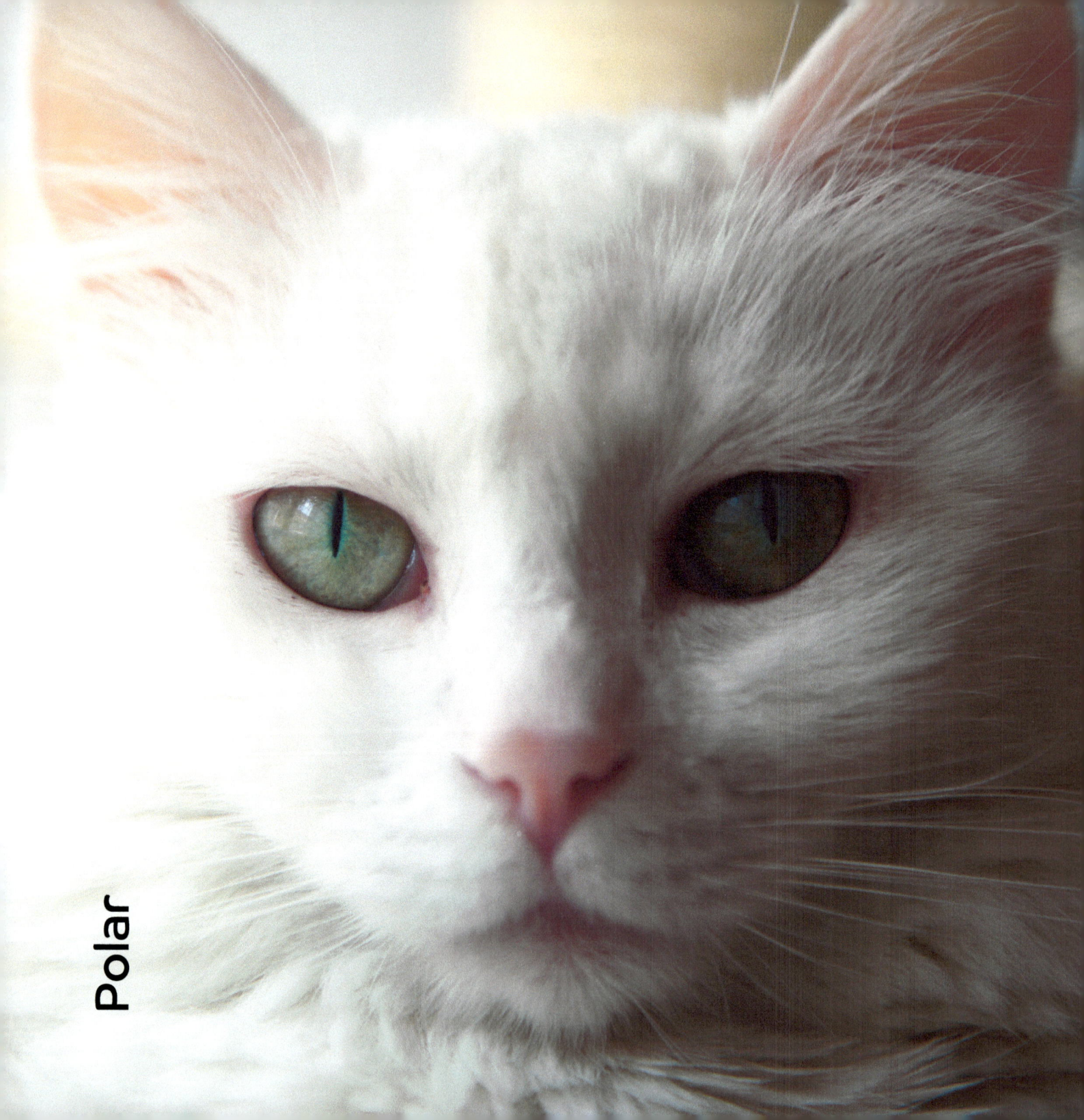

Polar

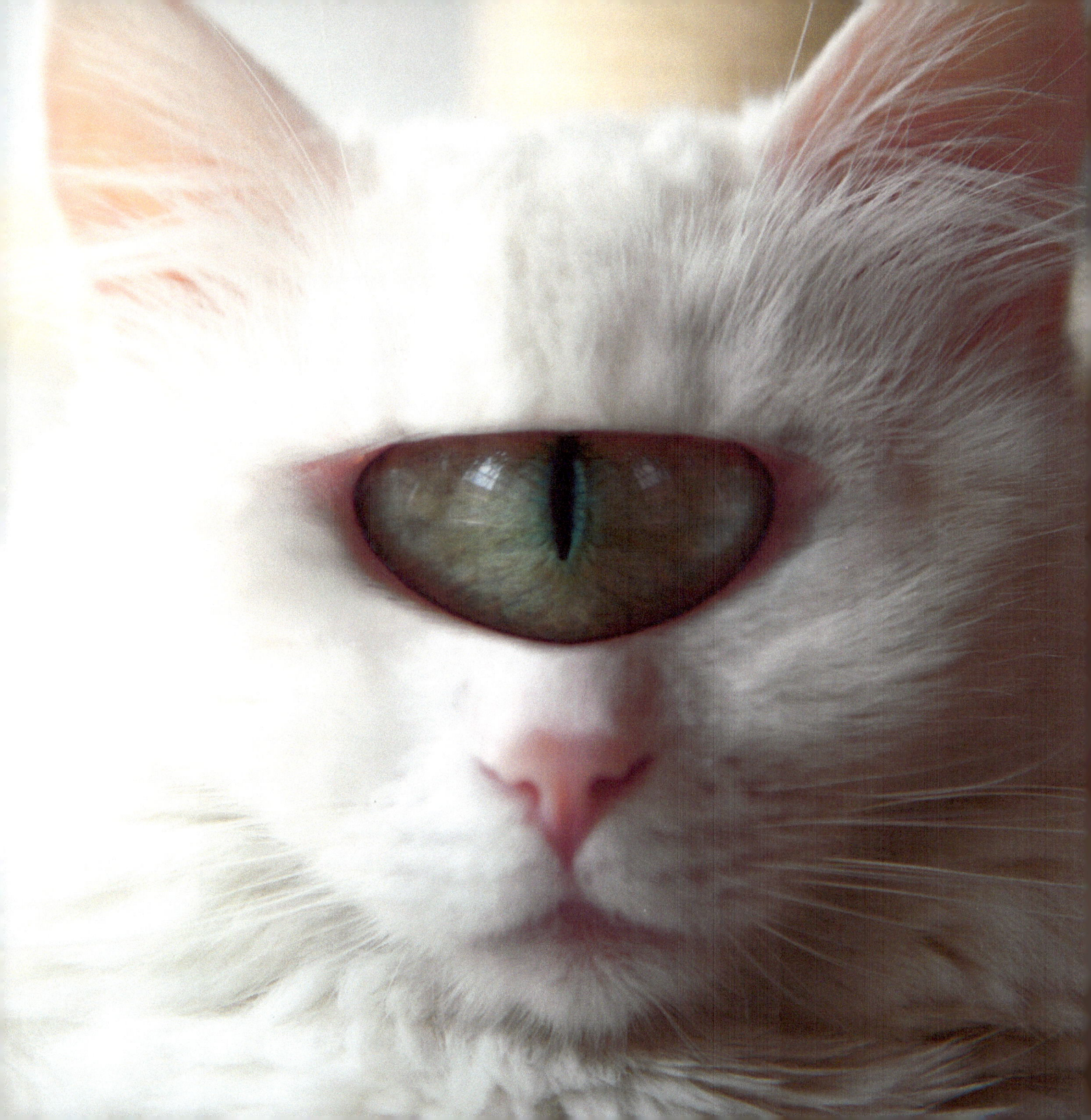

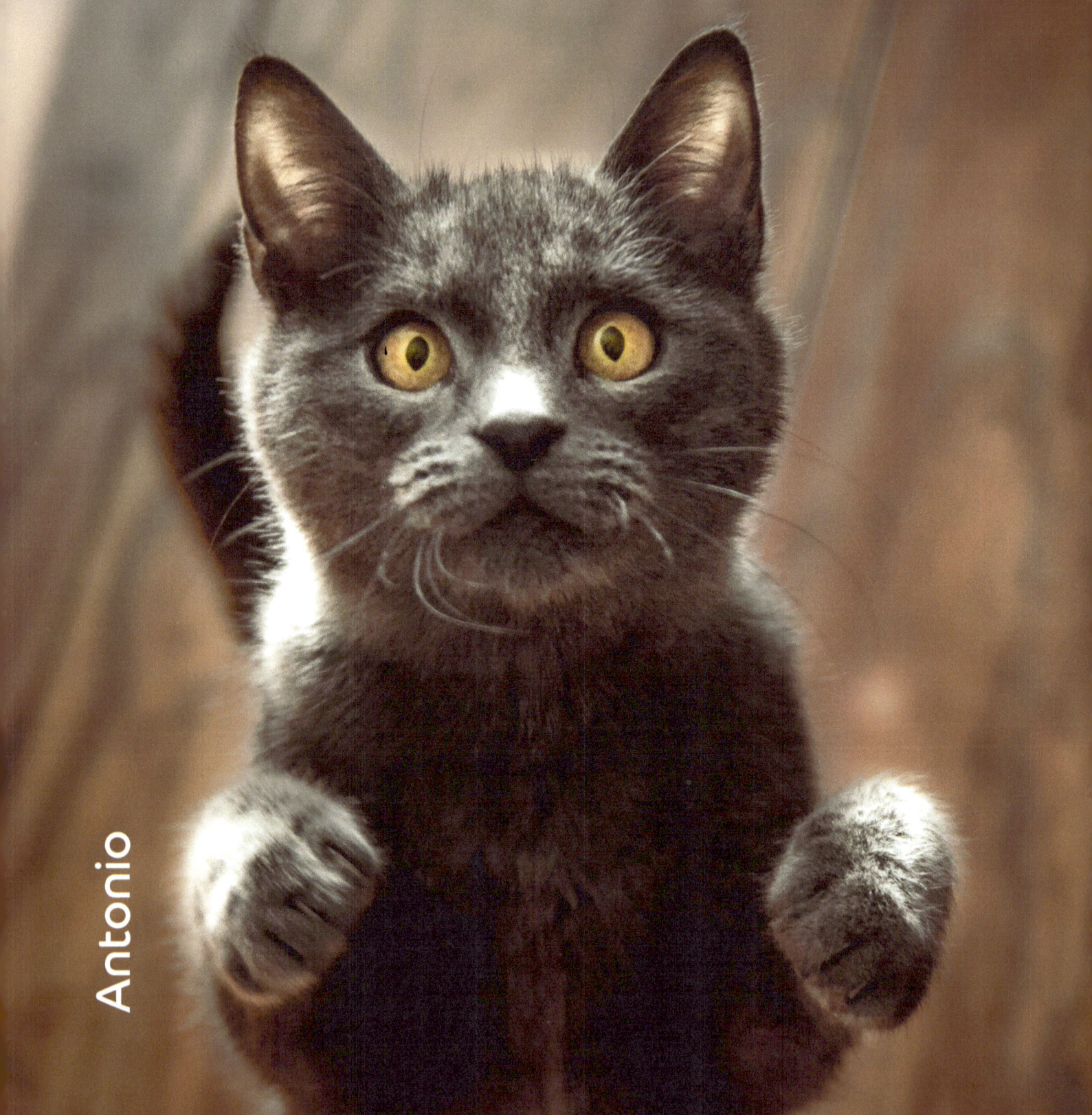

Antonio

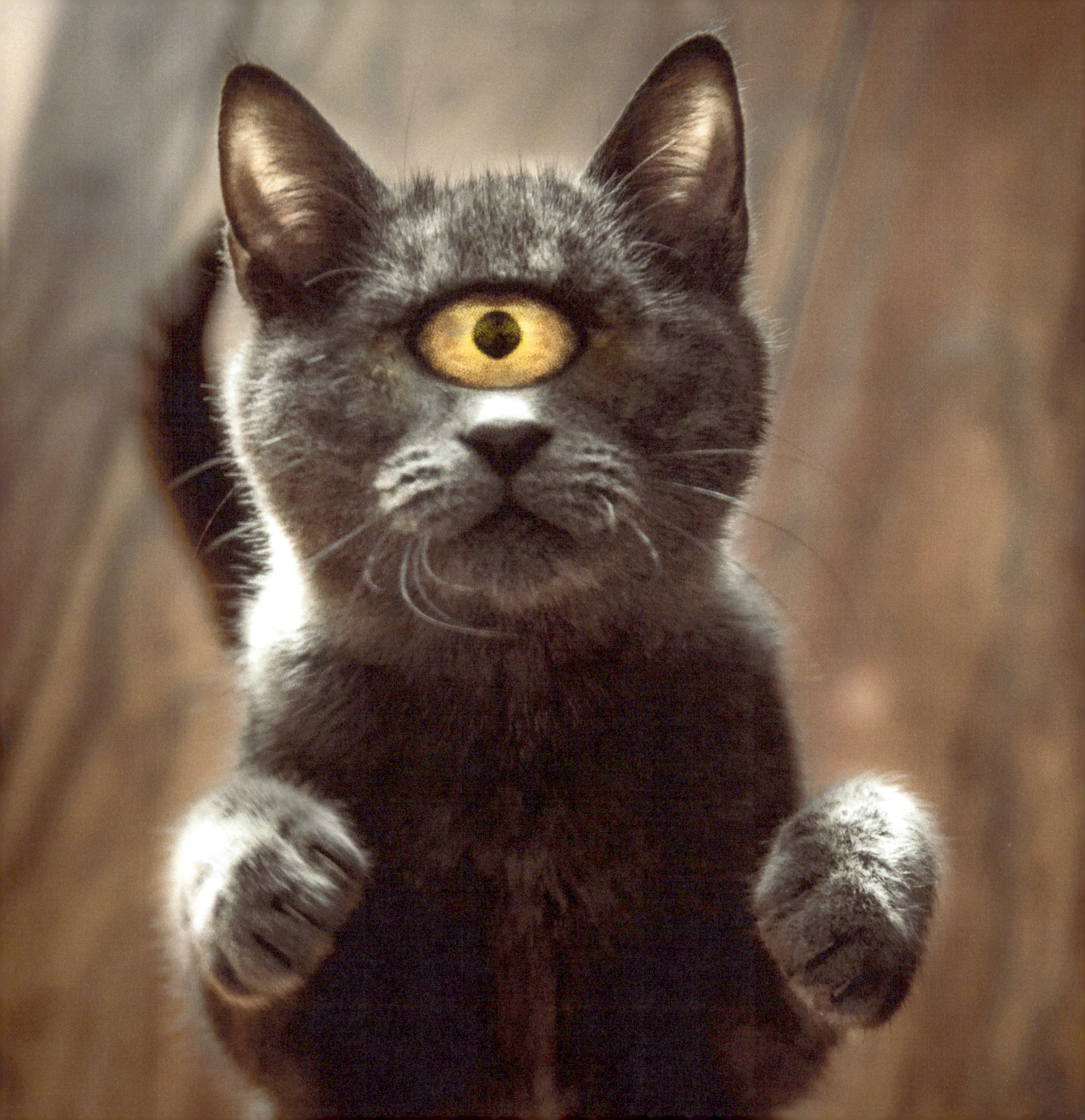

Dean Sinatra

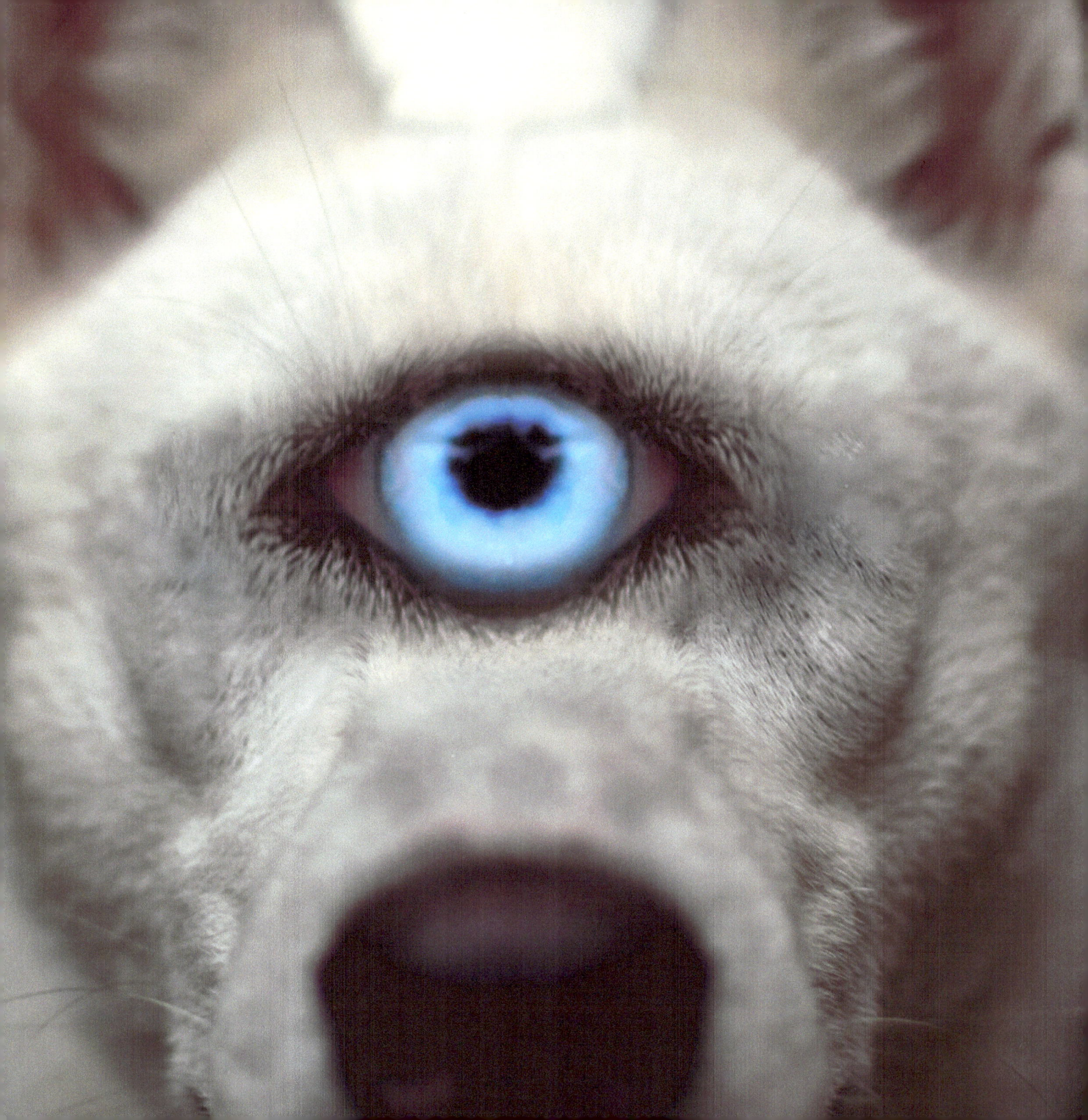

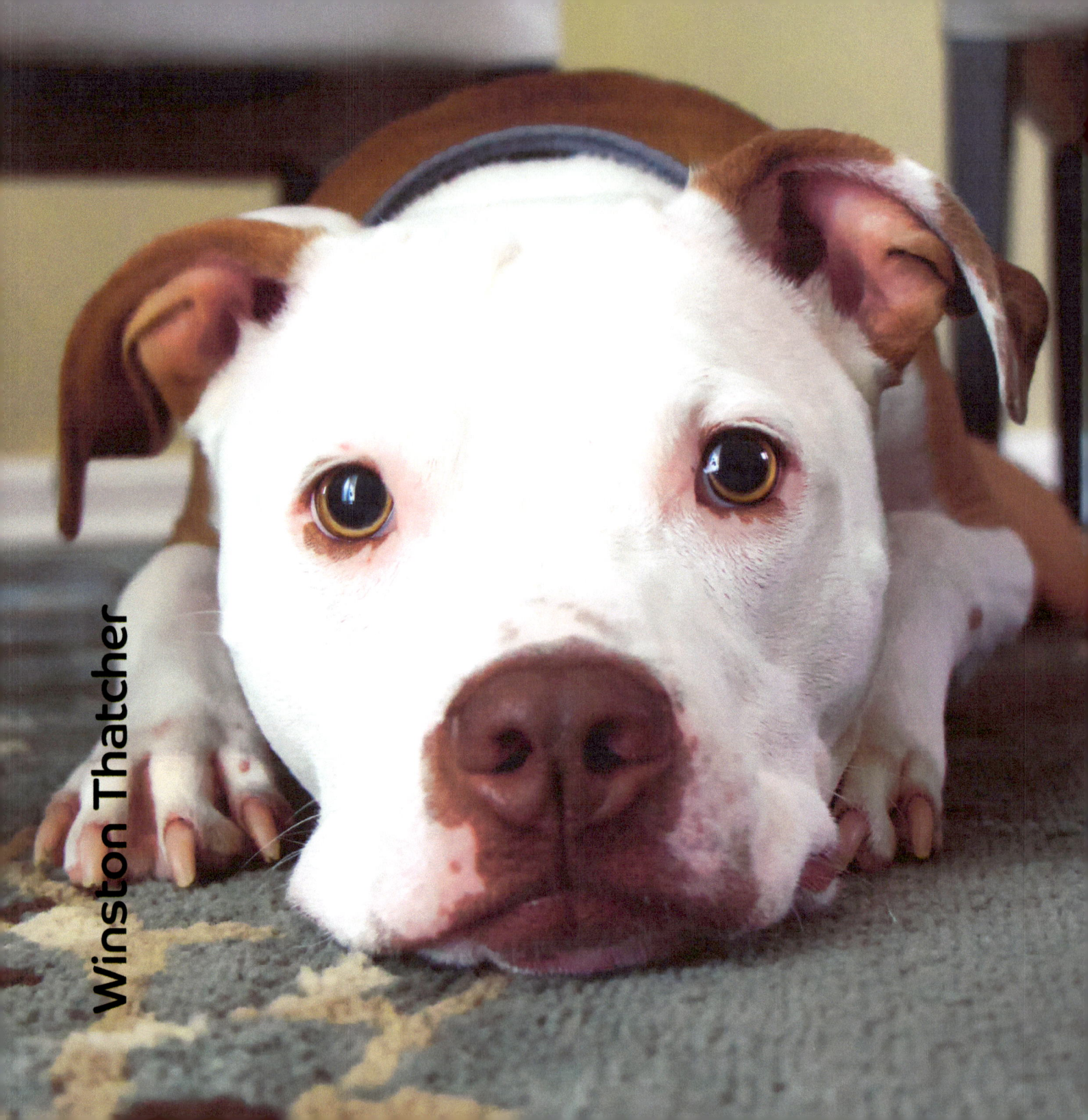

Winston Thatcher

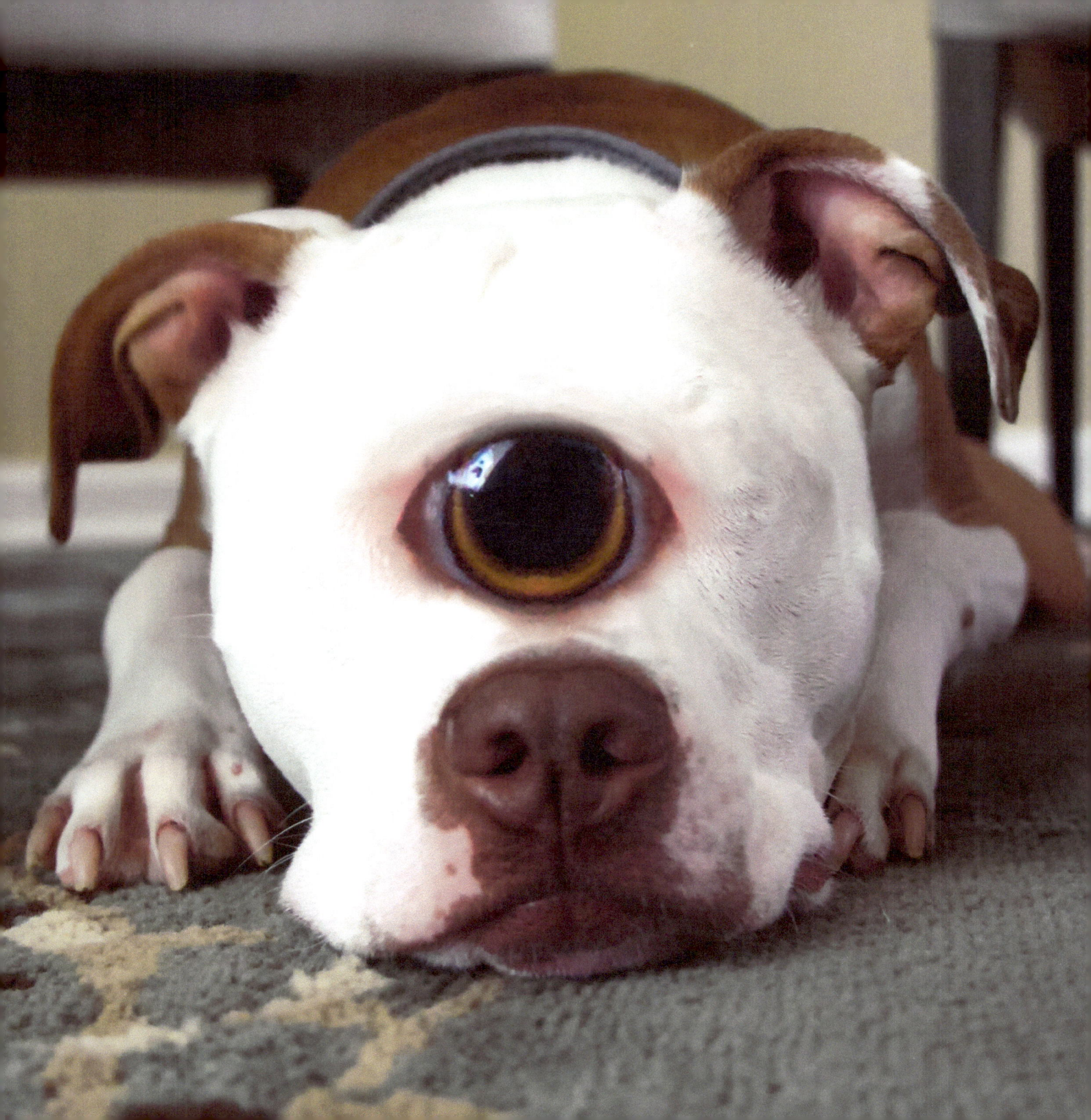

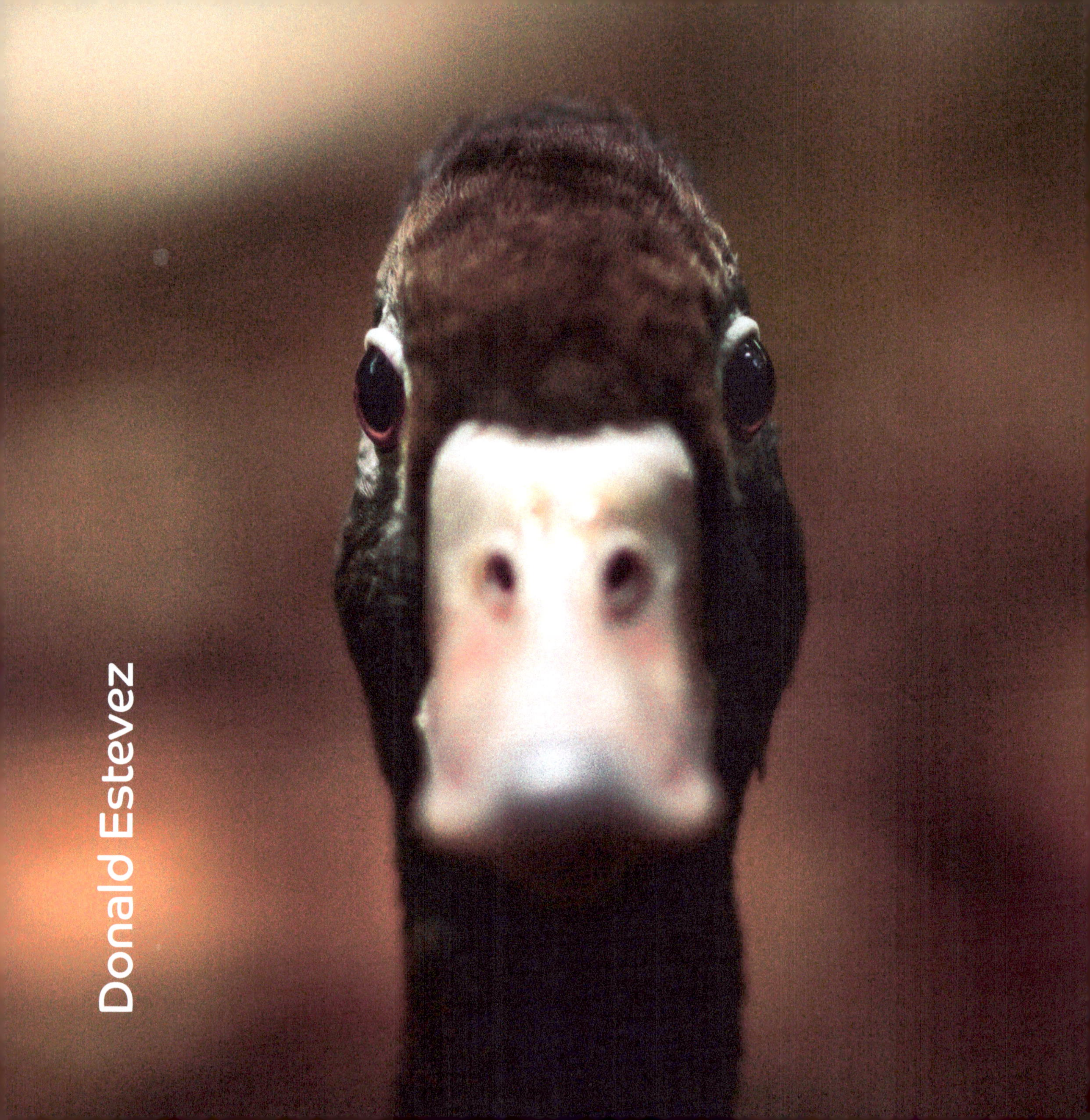
Donald Estevez

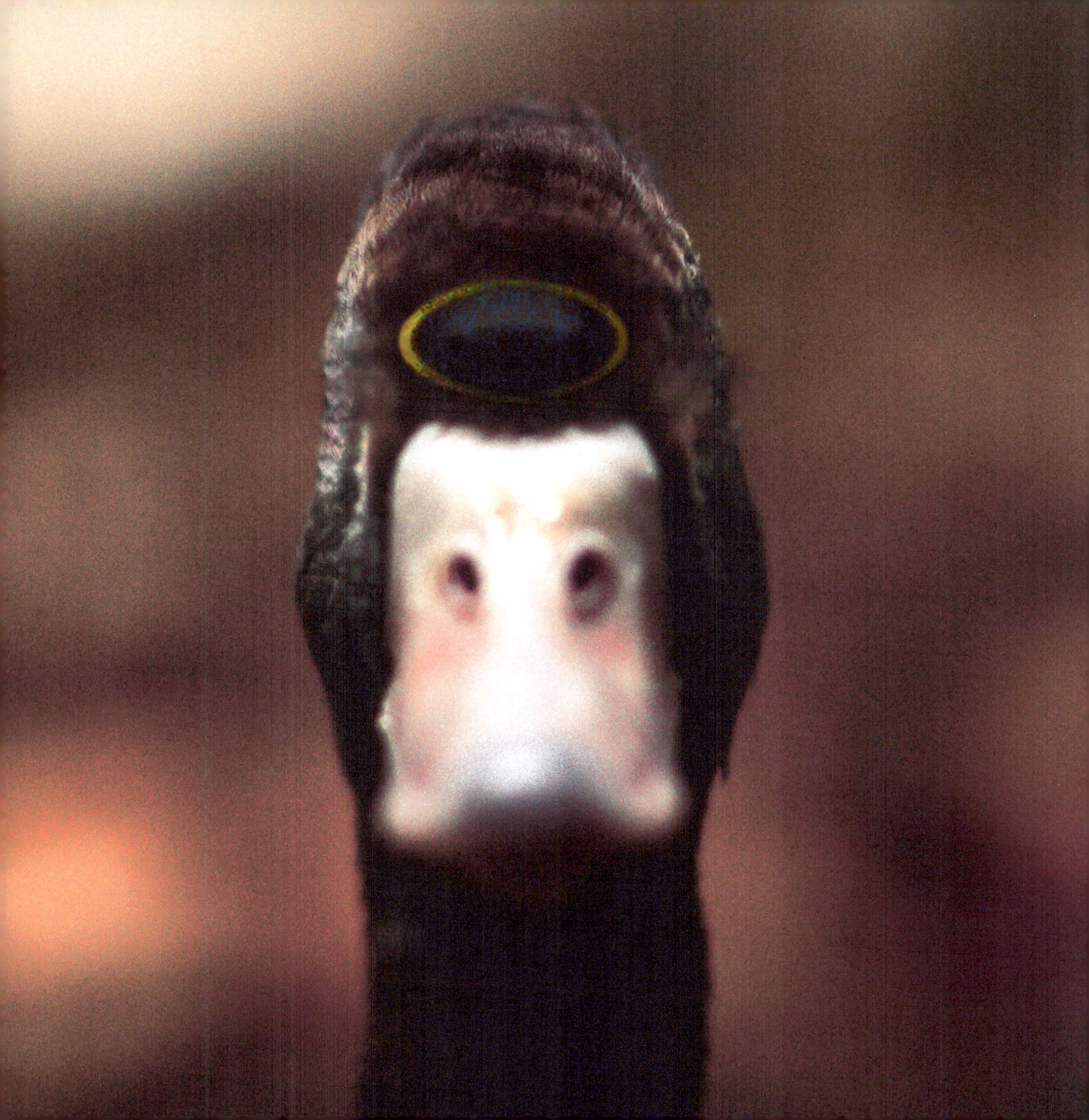

Beyoncé Carell

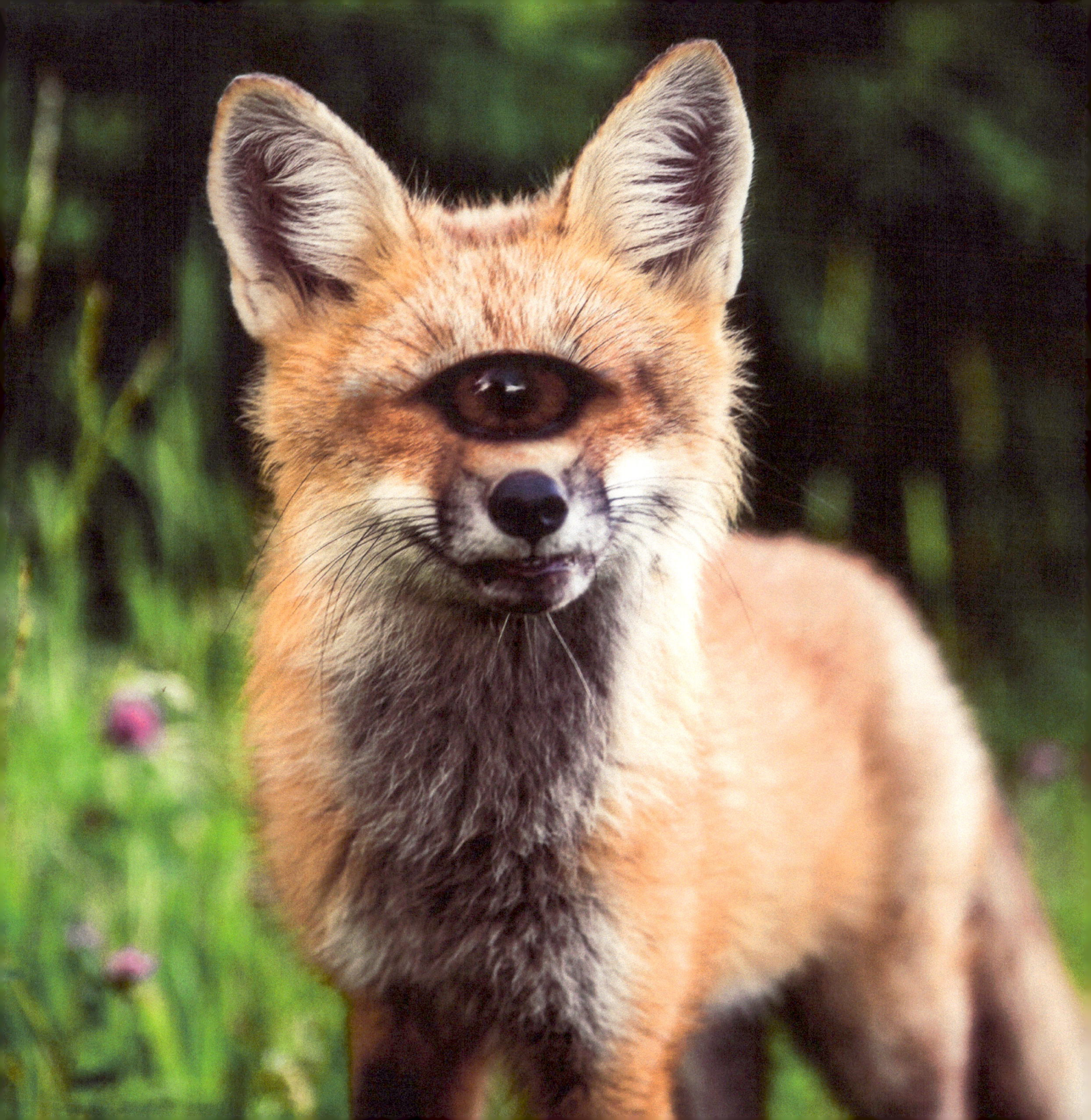

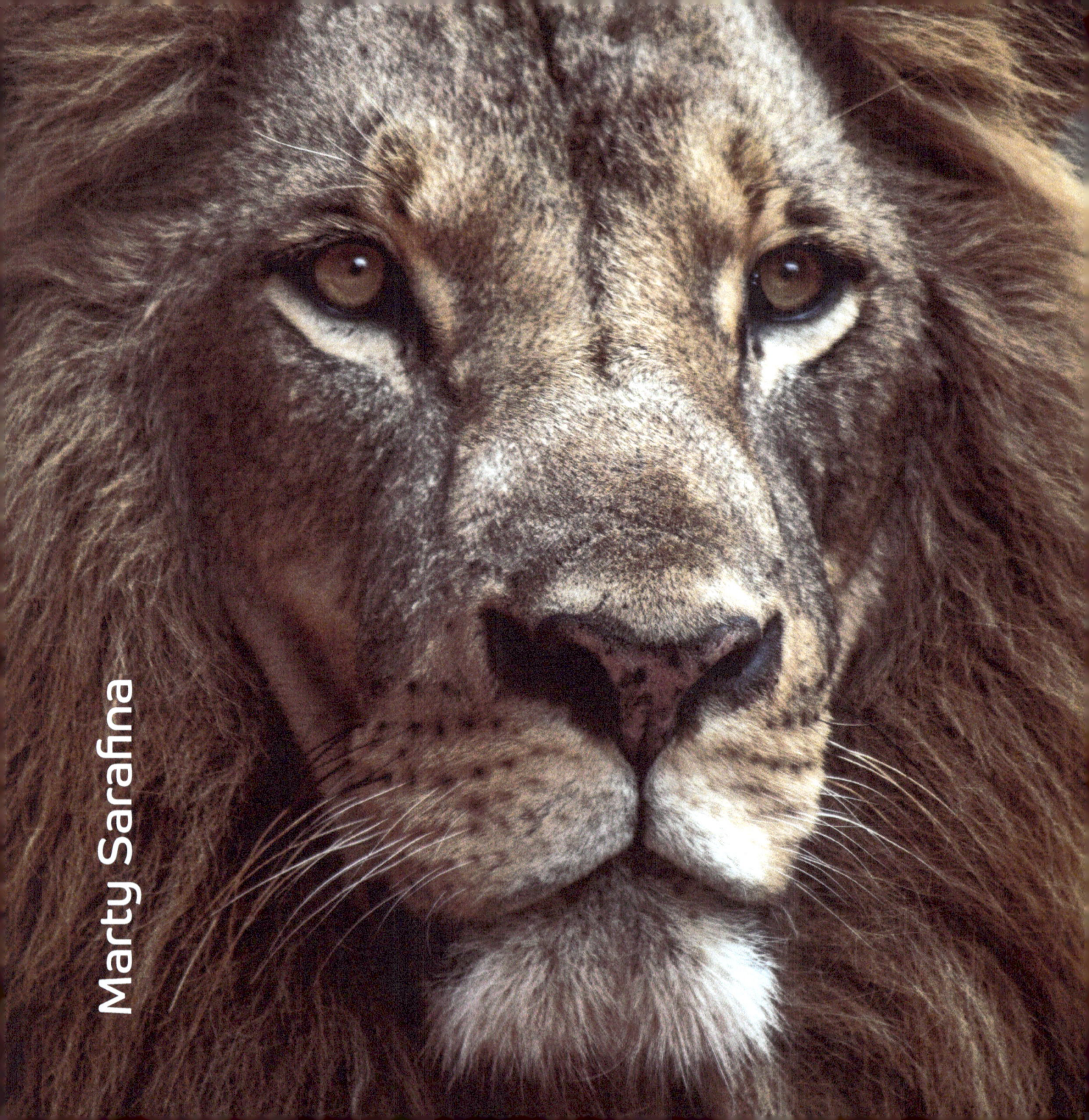

Marty Sarafina

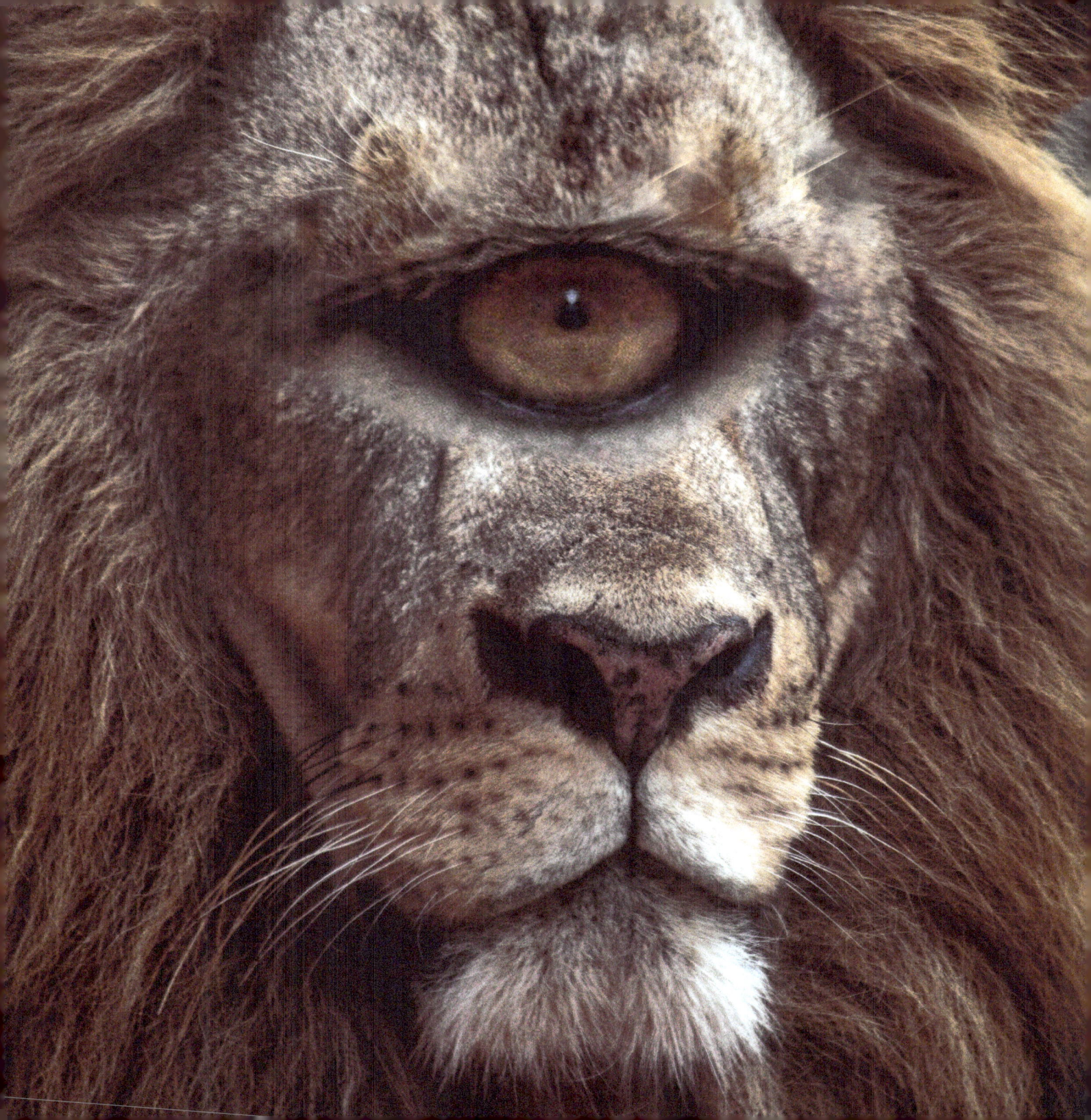

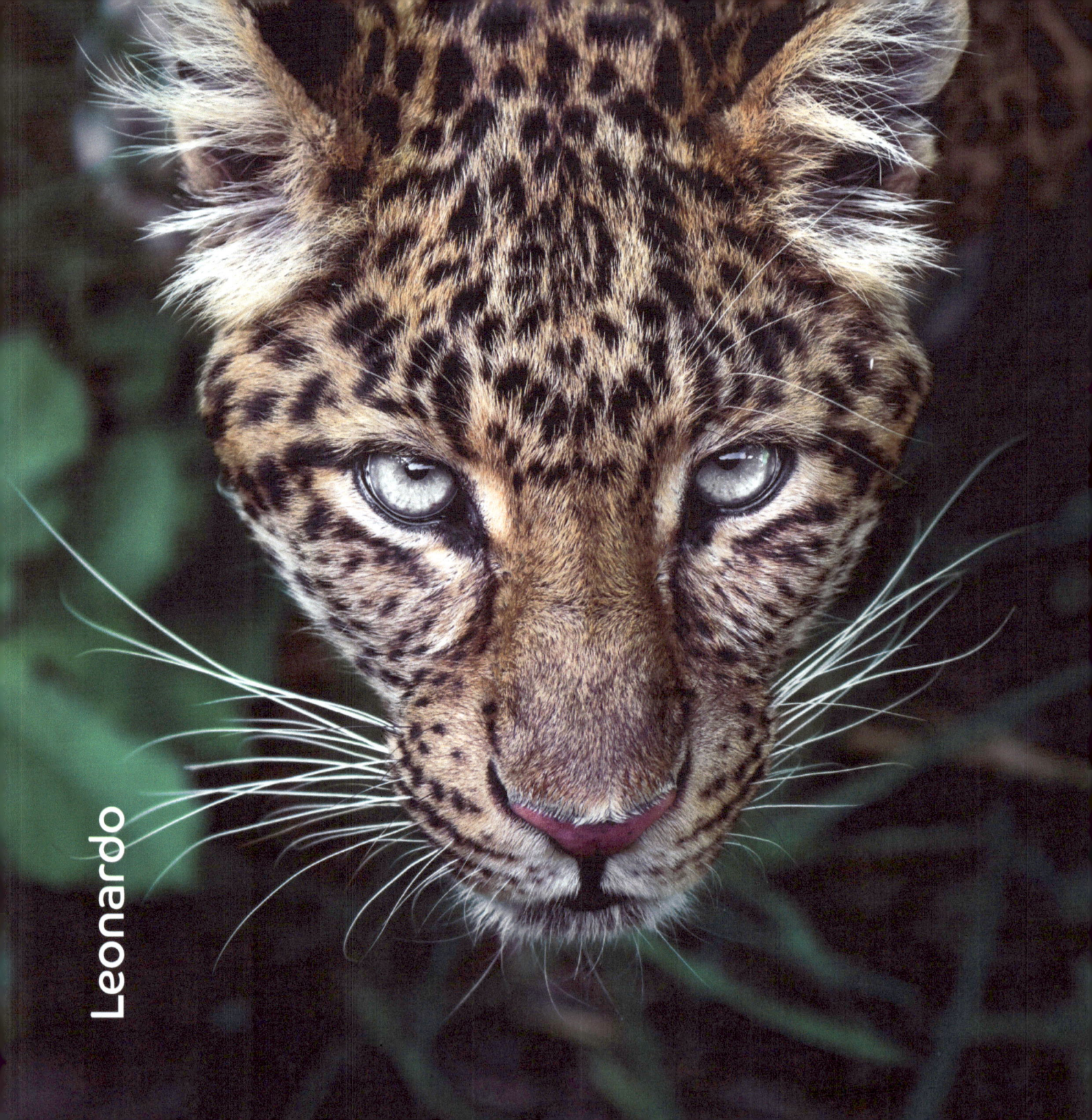

Leonardo

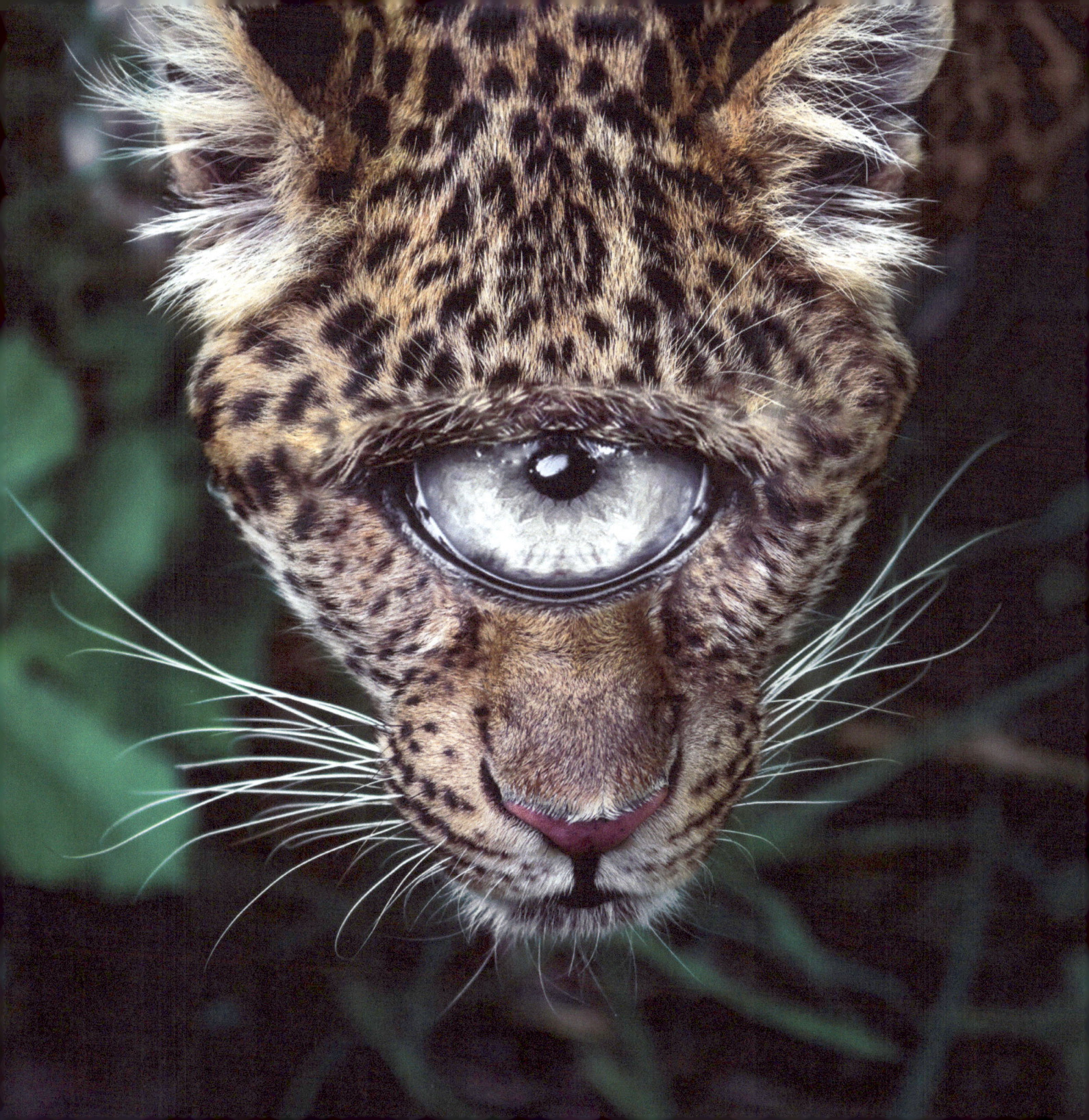

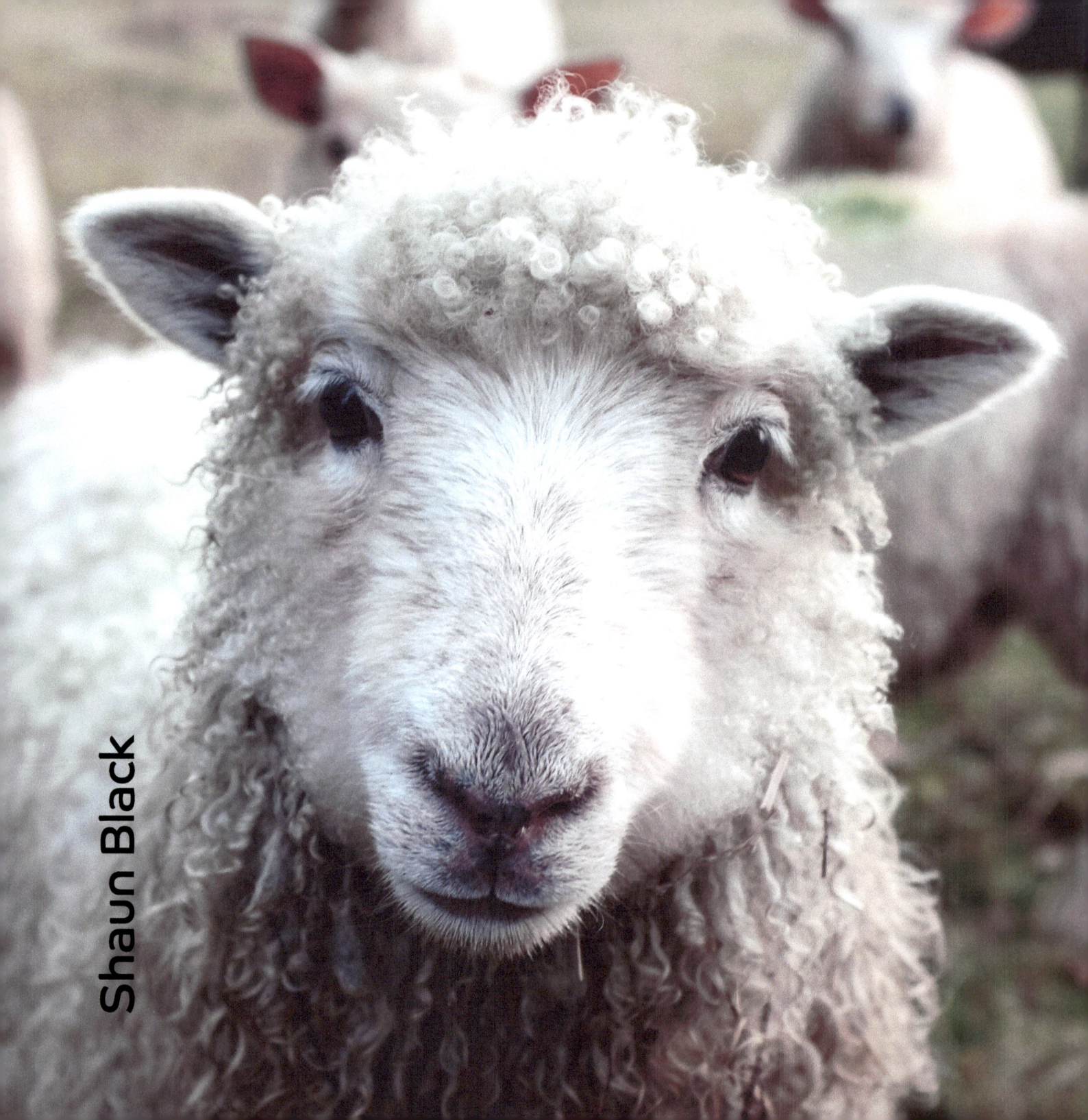

Shaun Black

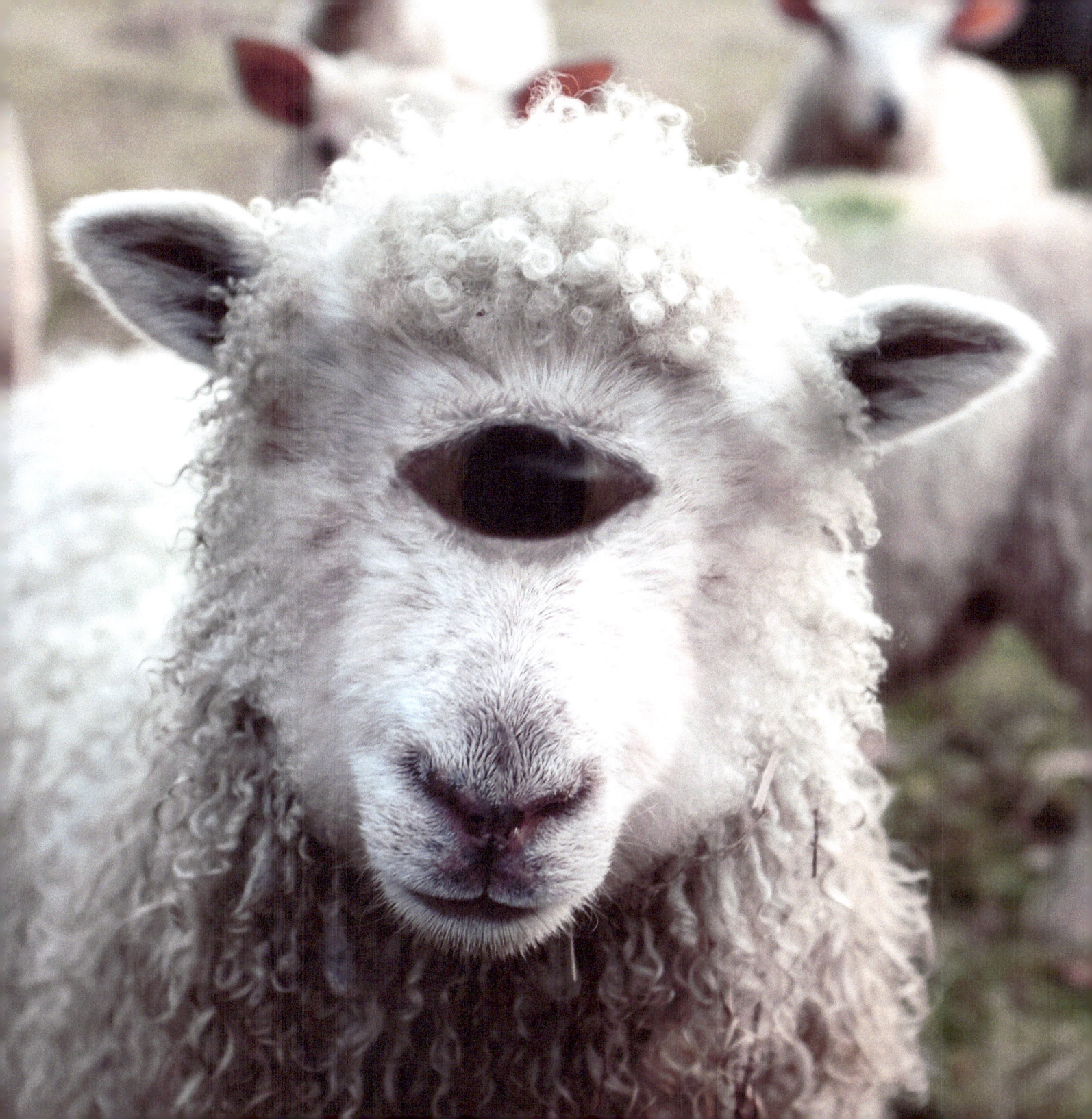

As a result of economic determinism and the ever growing trend of becoming a cyclop comes the growth of businesses to support the needs of people with one eye. Introducing the new specialised field of Cycloptometry.

Welcome to the

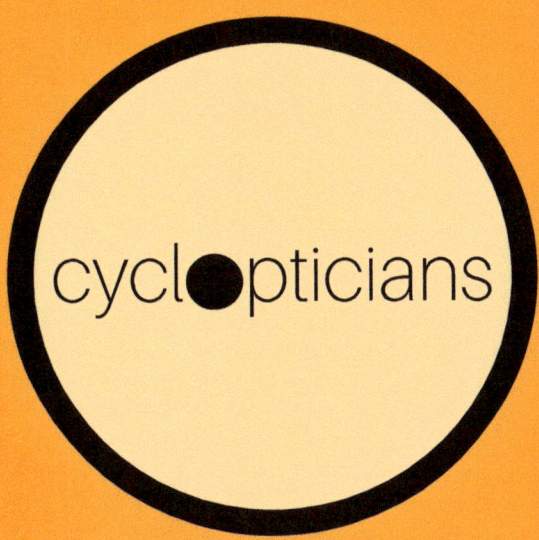

cyclopticians

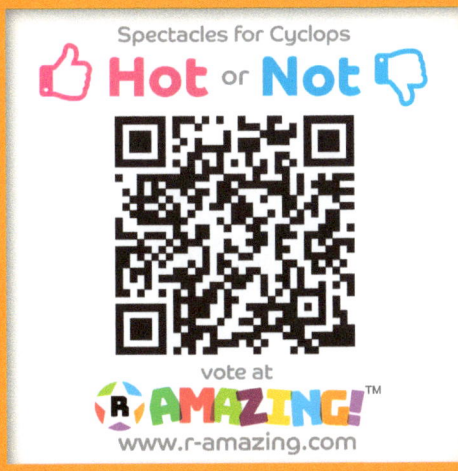

Spectacles for Cyclops
👍 Hot or Not 👎

vote at
R·AMAZING!™
www.r-amazing.com

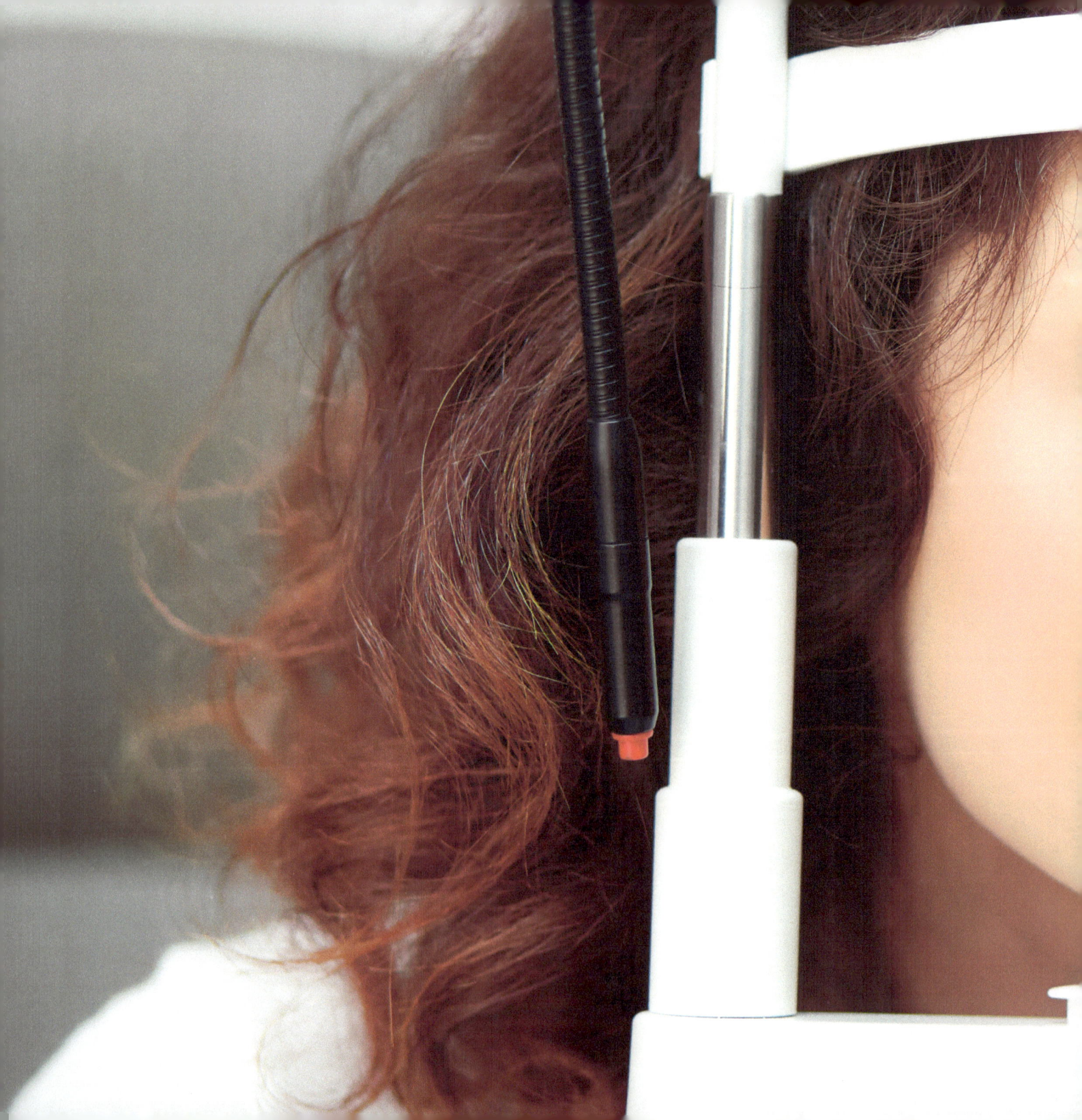

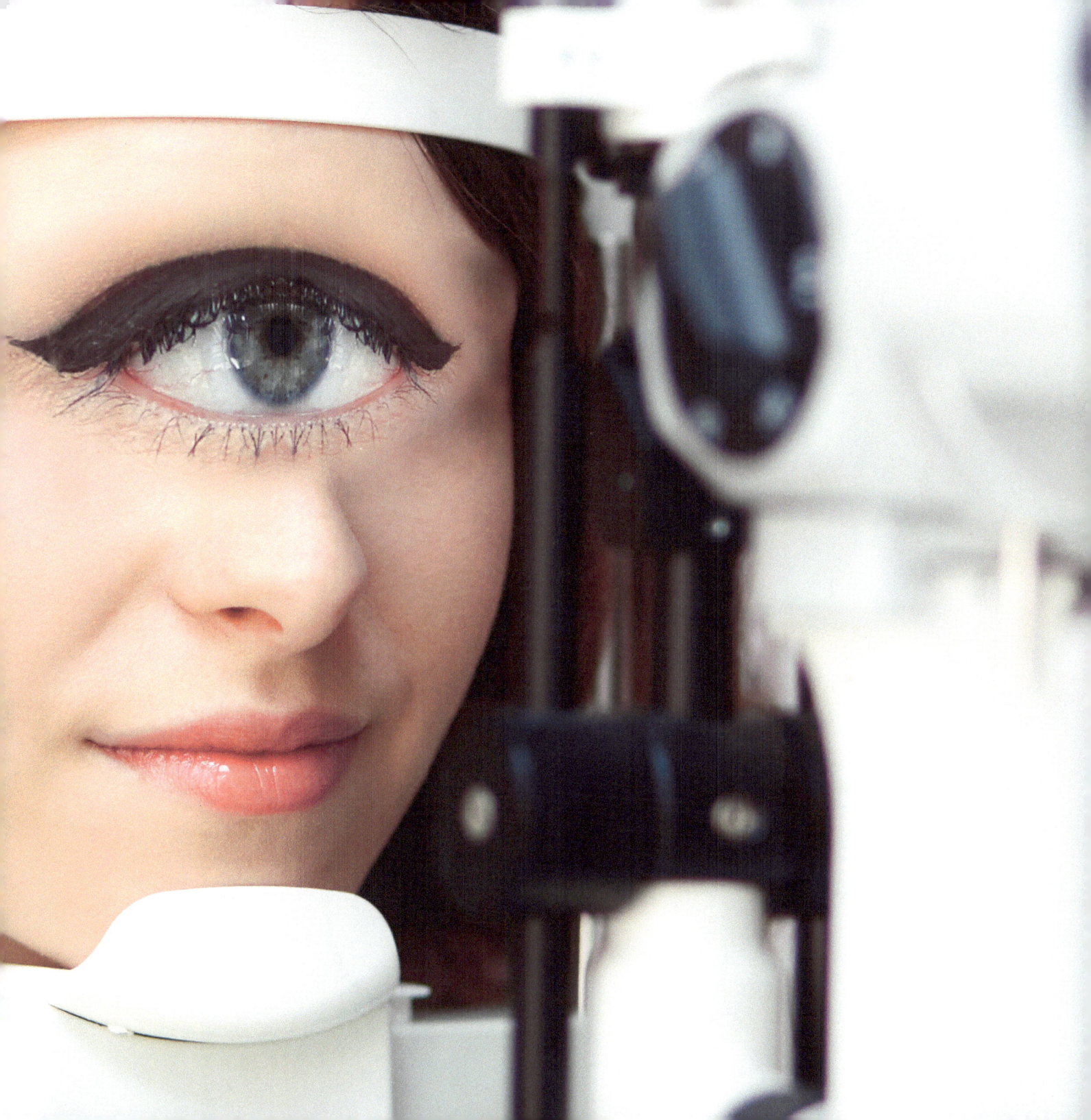

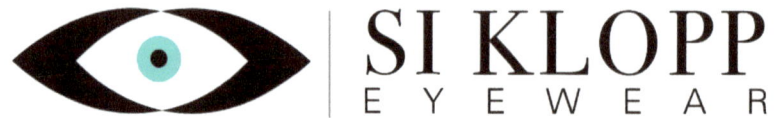

SI KLOPP
E Y E W E A R

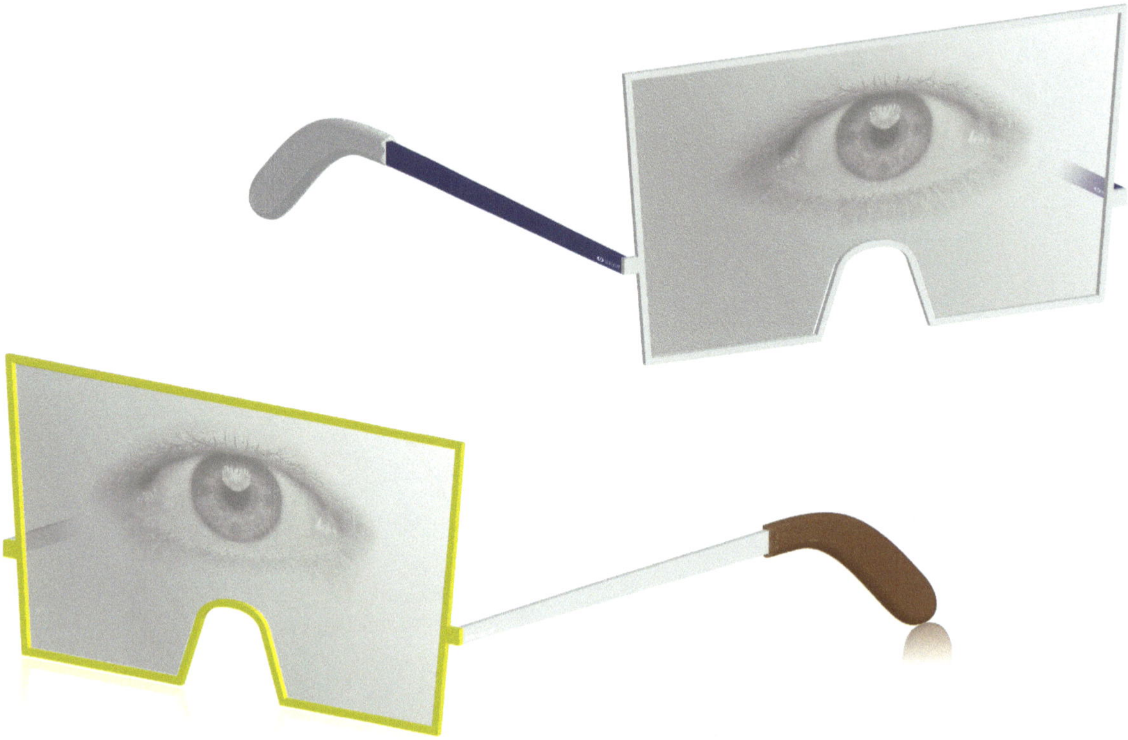

BIRDS EYE

Exclusively available at the cyclopticians

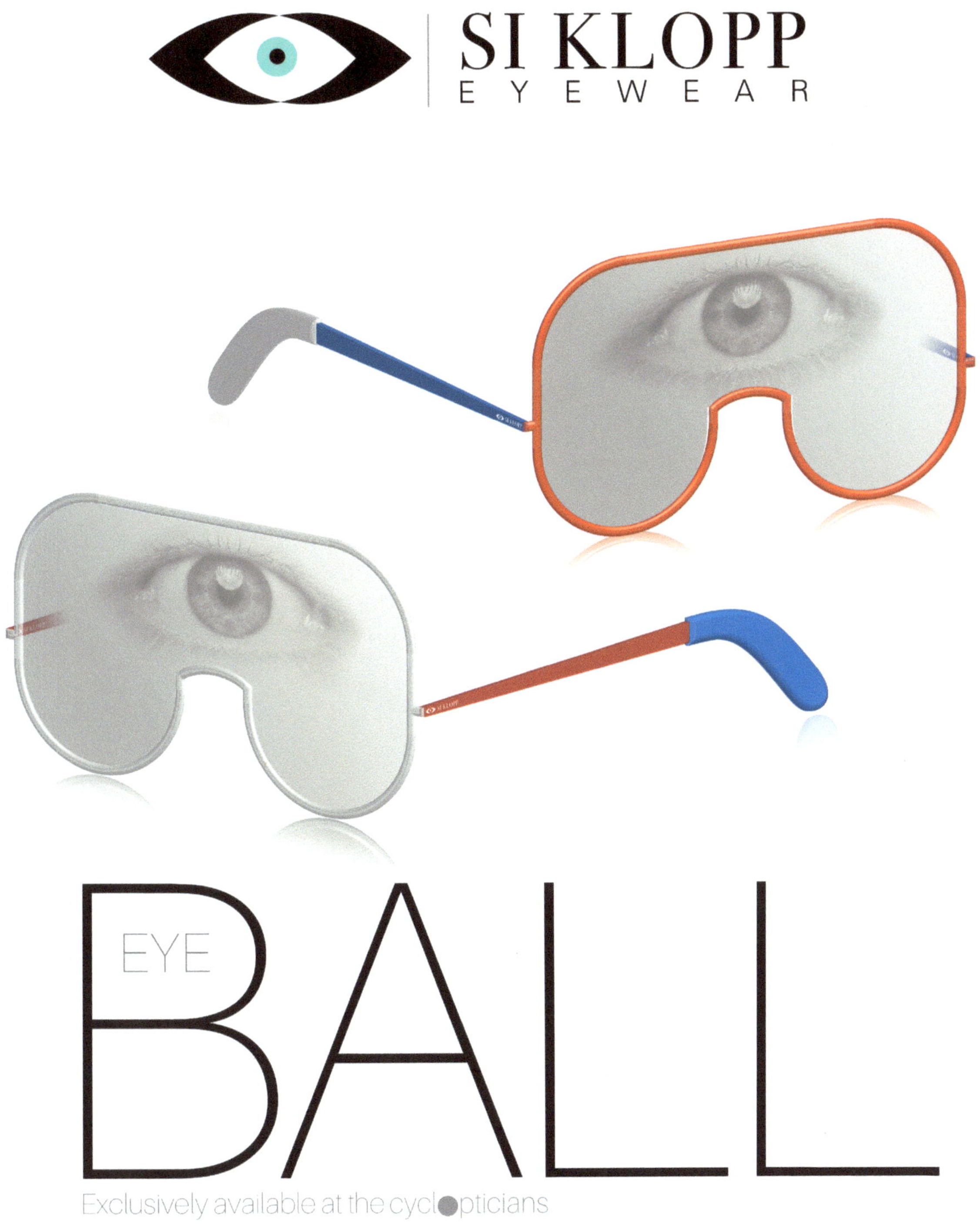

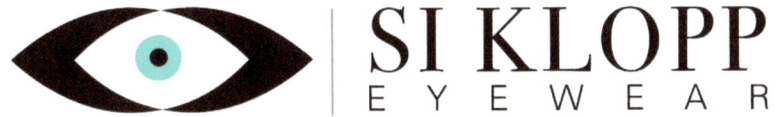

SI KLOPP
EYEWEAR

EYE
BALL

Exclusively available at the cyclopticians

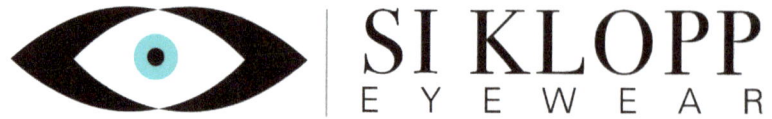

SI KLOPP
EYEWEAR

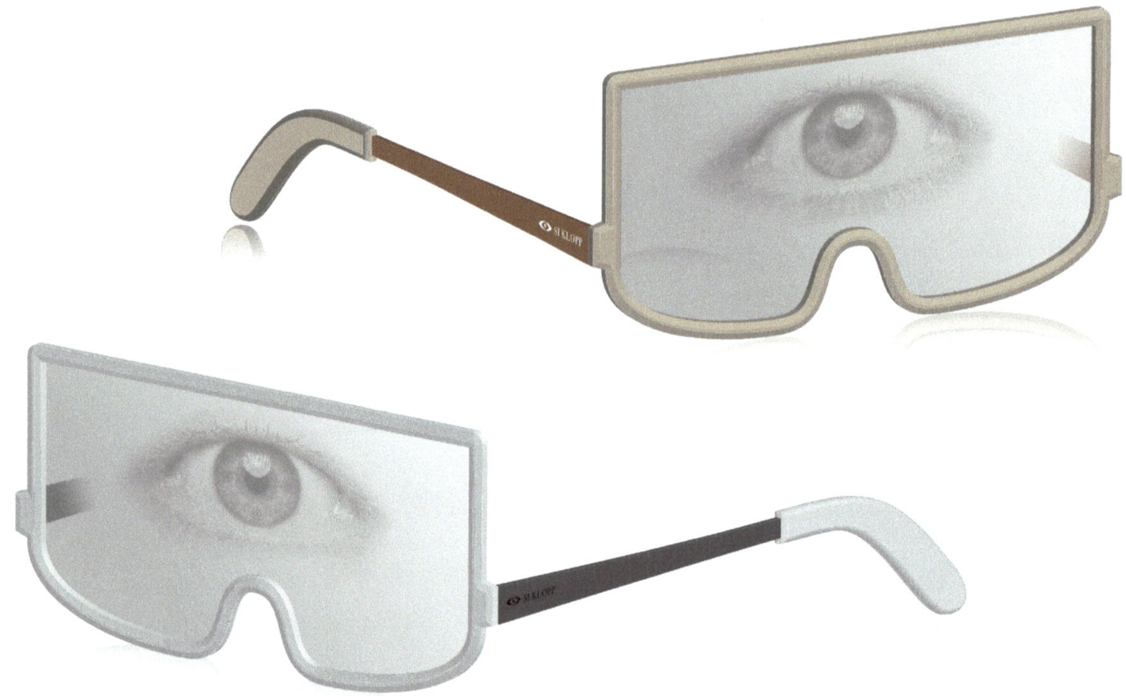

EYE FULL

Exclusively available at the cyclopticians

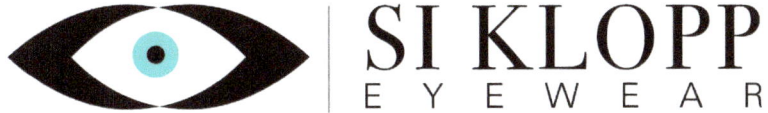

SI KLOPP
E Y E W E A R

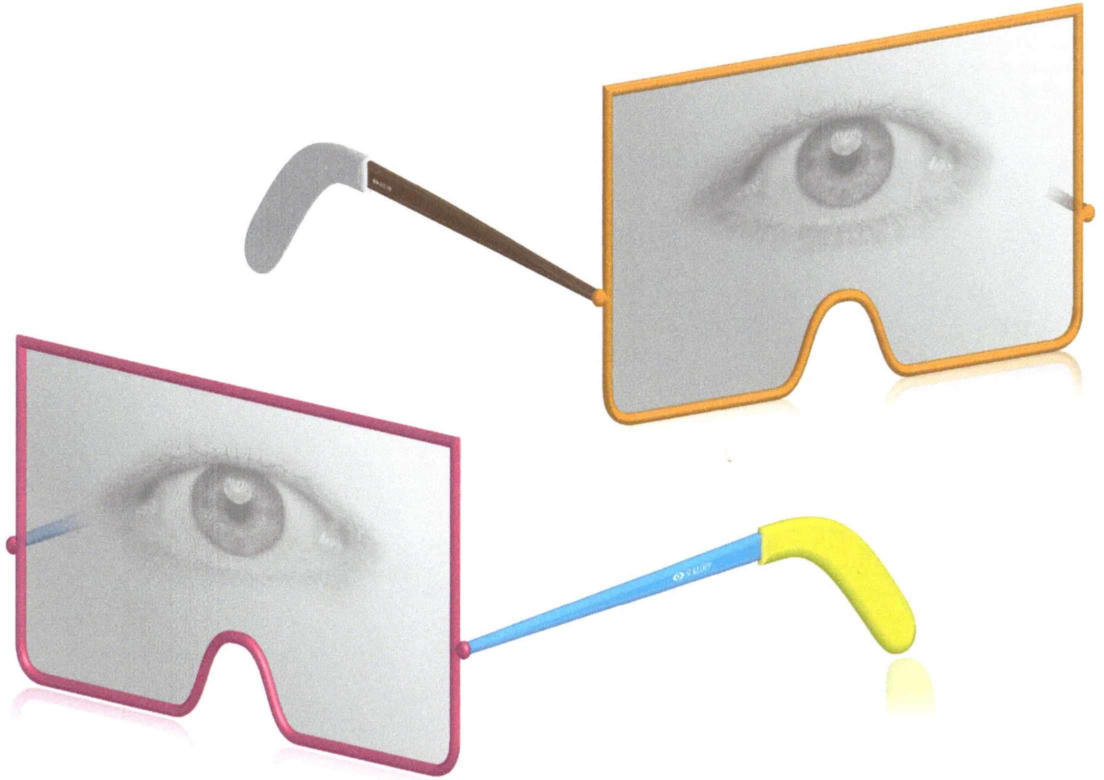

EYE DROPS

Exclusively available at the cycl⬤pticians

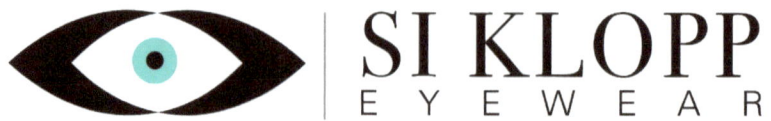

SI KLOPP
E Y E W E A R

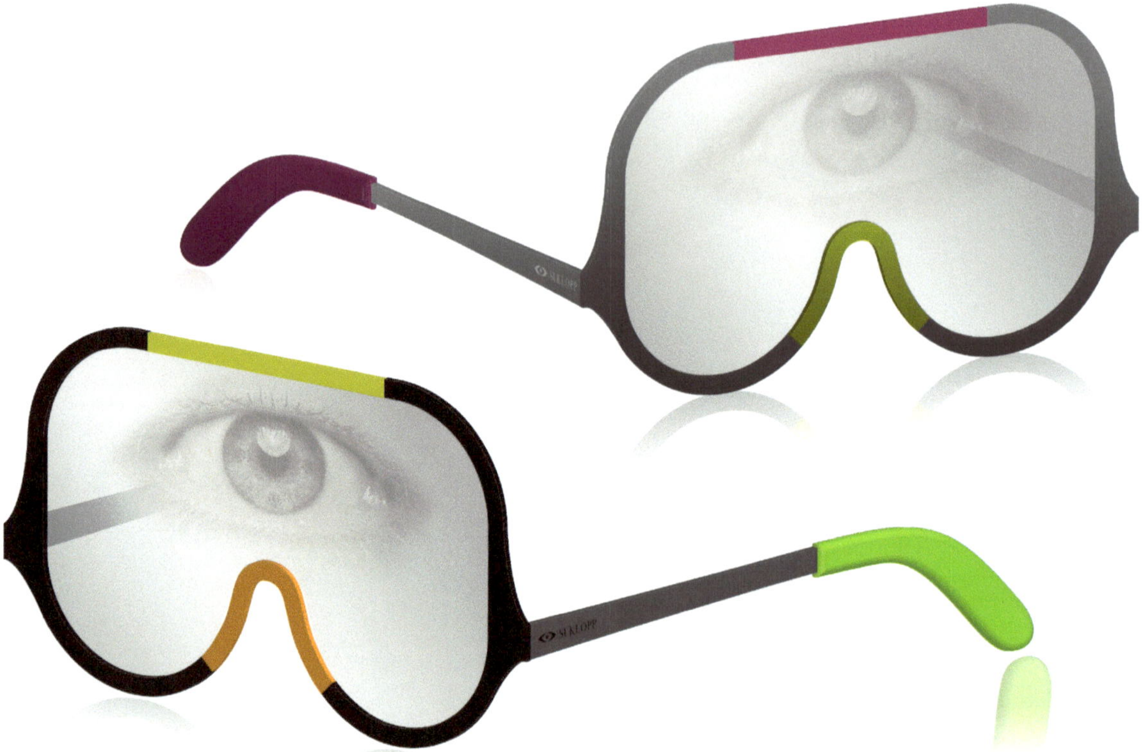

POP EYE

Exclusively available at the cyclopticians

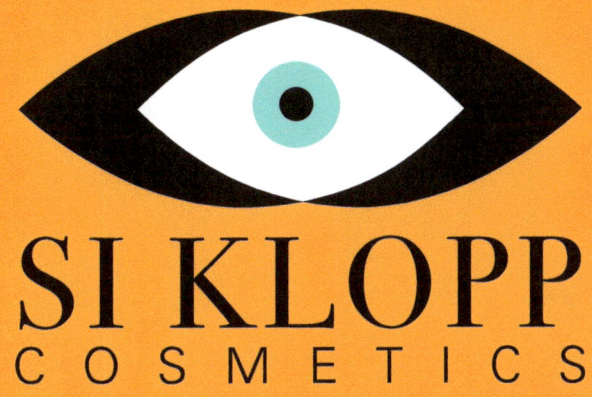

SI KLOPP
C O S M E T I C S

Makeup for those with
an eye for improvement.

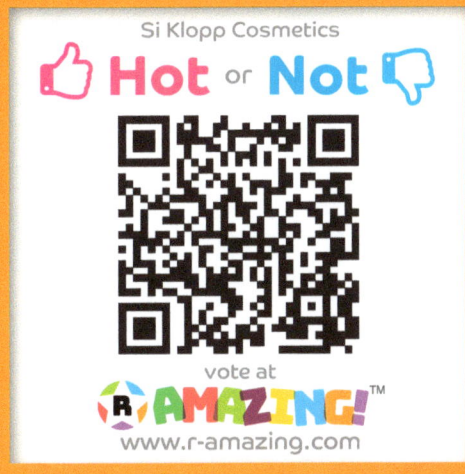

Si Klopp Cosmetics

👍 Hot or Not 👎

vote at
R AMAZING!™
www.r-amazing.com

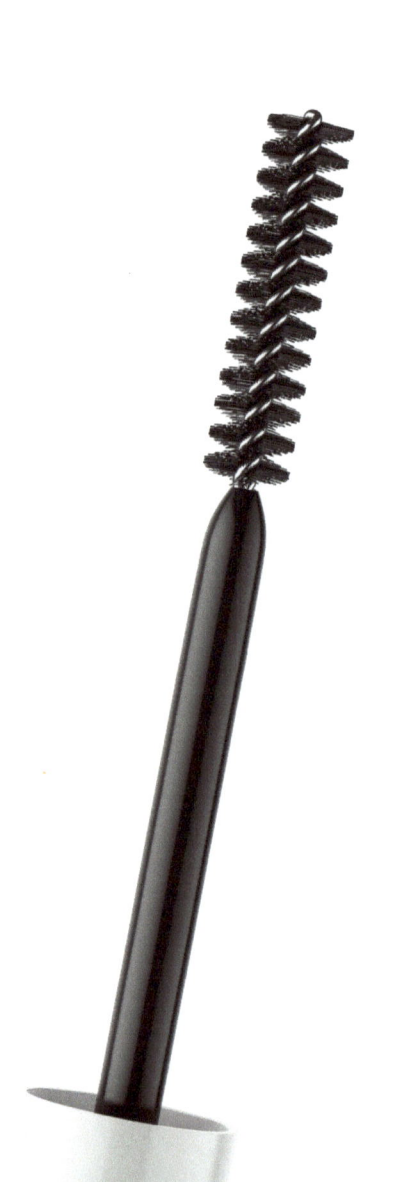
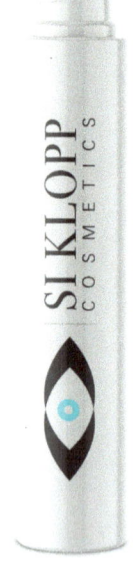
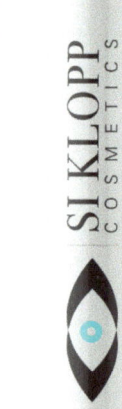

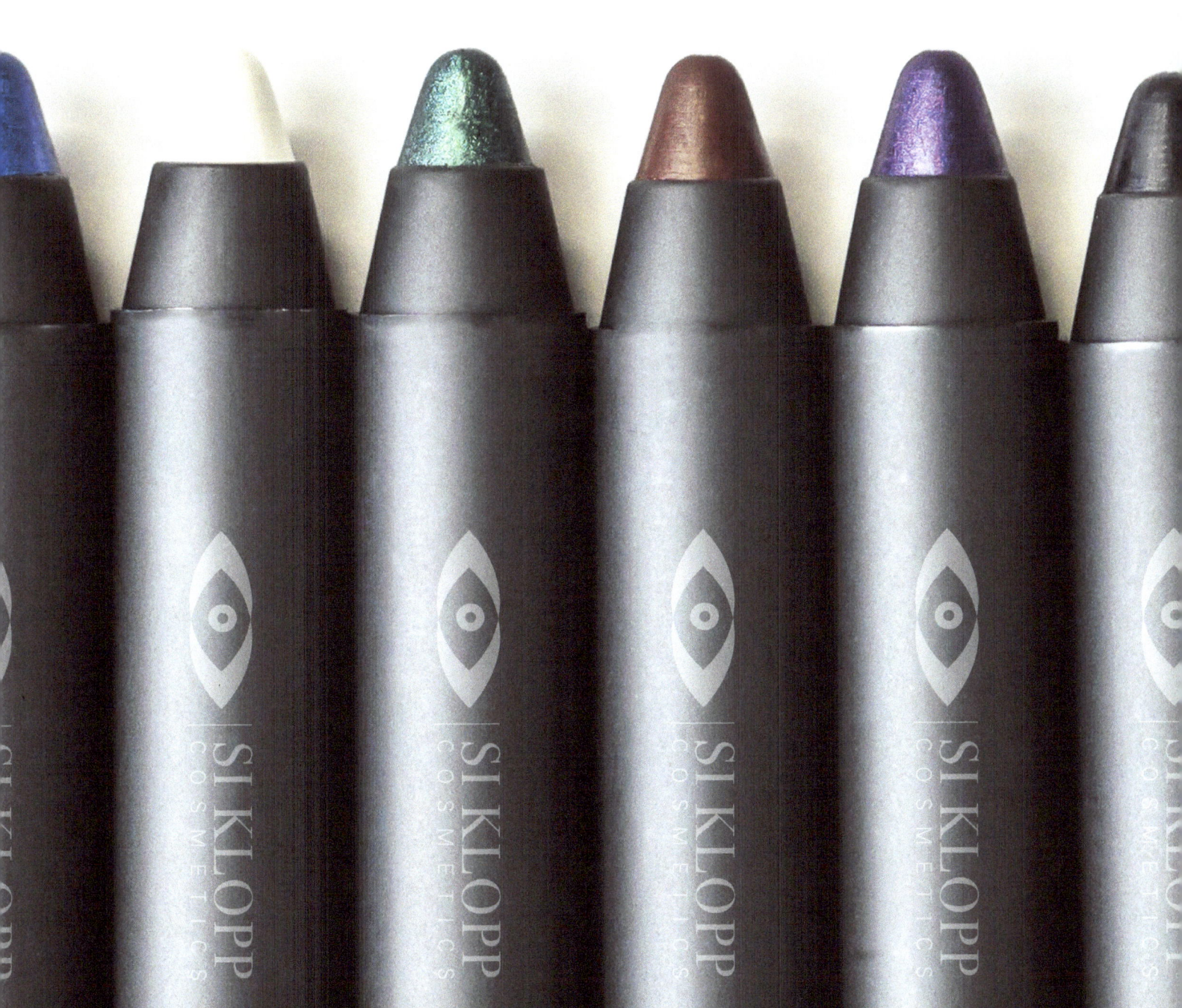

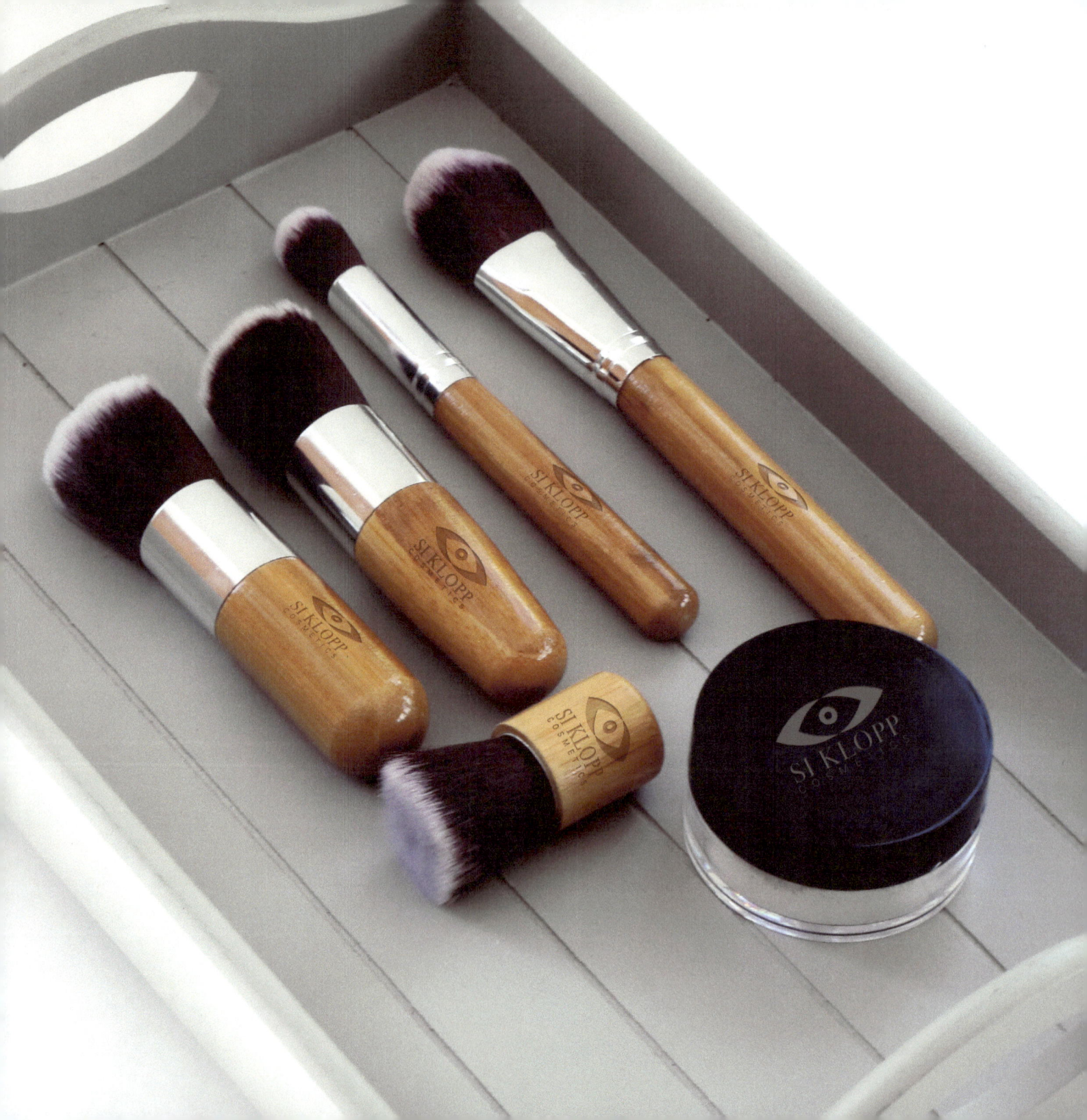

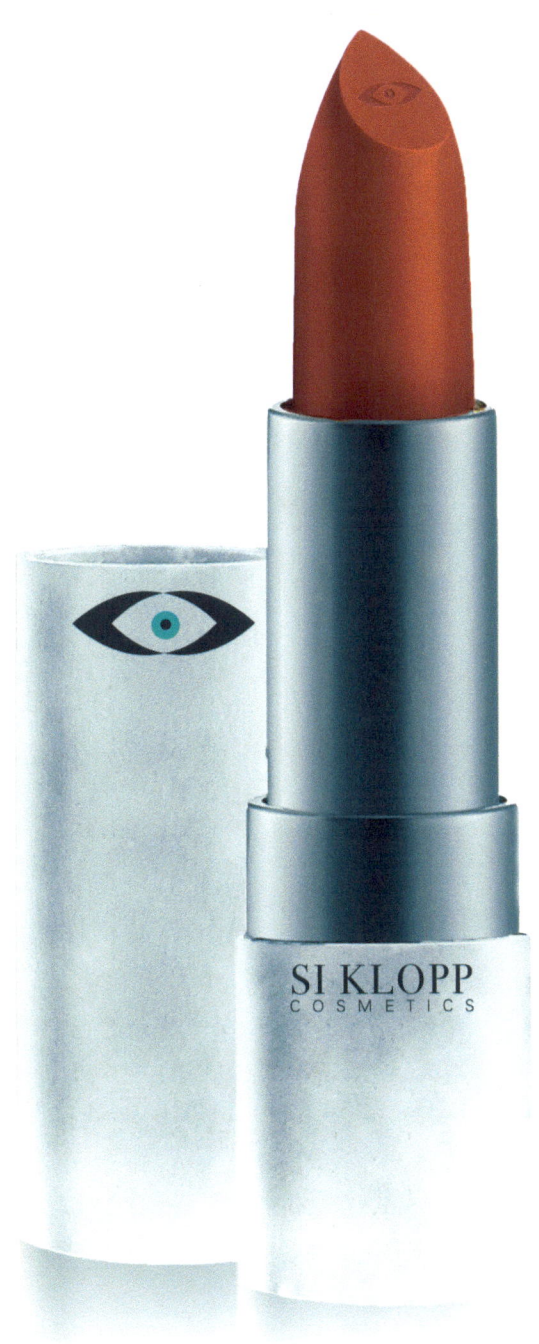

SI KLOPP
COSMETICS

Many people ask what inspired the 'Cycloped' Eye Reduction Surgery to be developed. The answer may surprise you.

Professor Klopp has always had a love for finding faces in everyday objects called Pareidolia, which led her to find the creative work of Markus Baker.

What Markus did next changed the lives of many people, including Simone's, forever. For Markus started to find cycloptic faces in everyday objects and turned these into quirky characters. These characters were to inspire the creation of the 'Cycloped' Eye Reduction Surgery.

Say hello to the

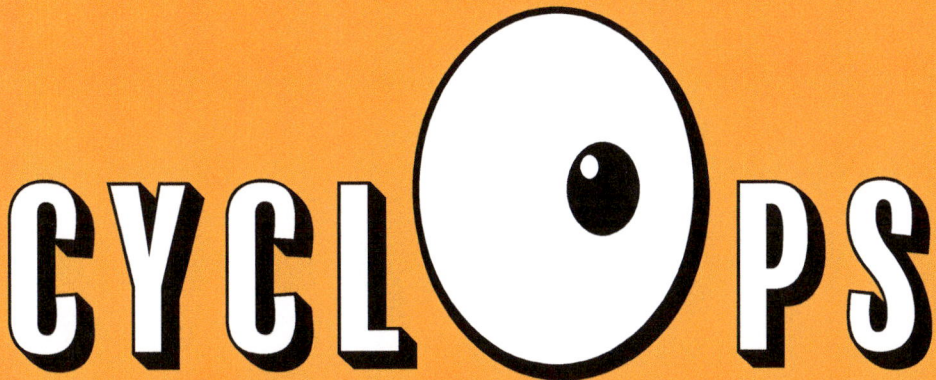

CYCLOPS

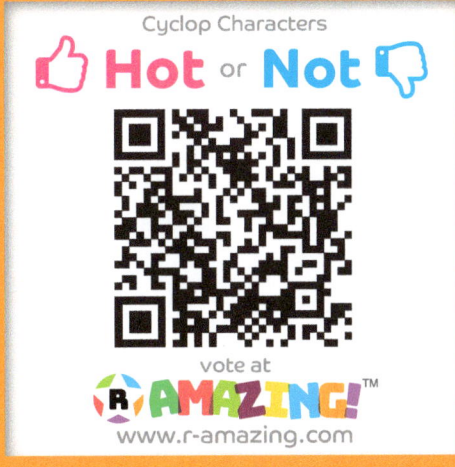

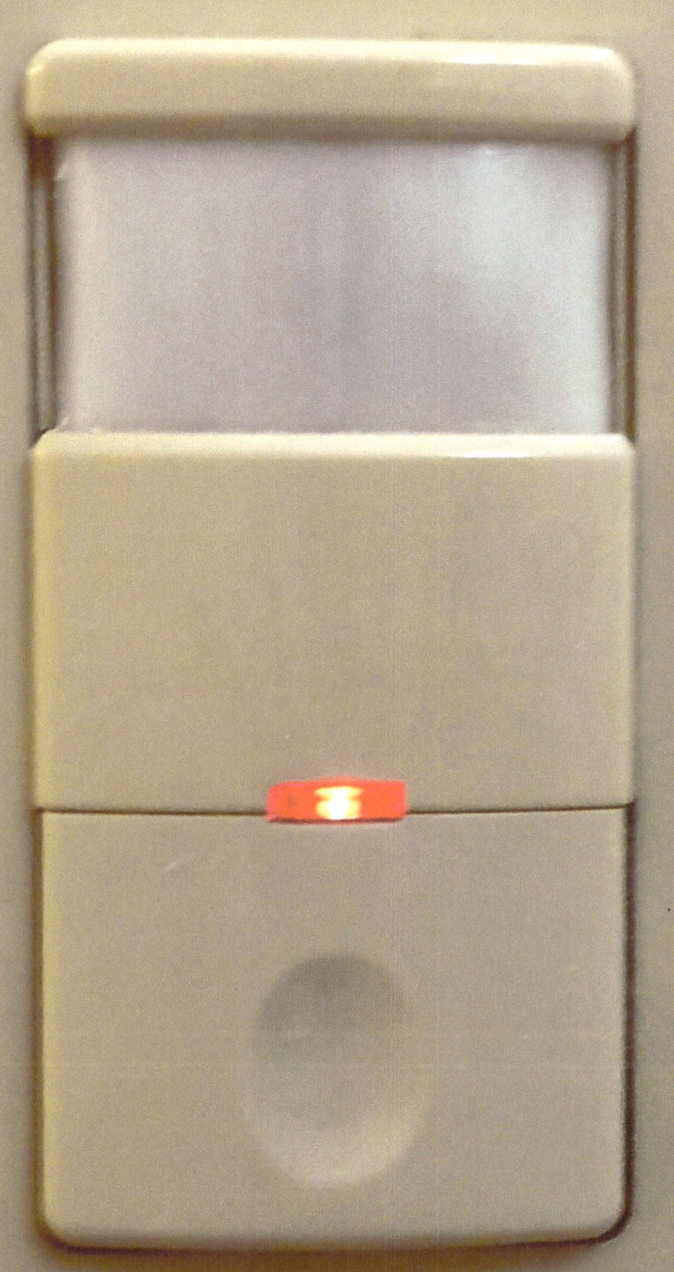
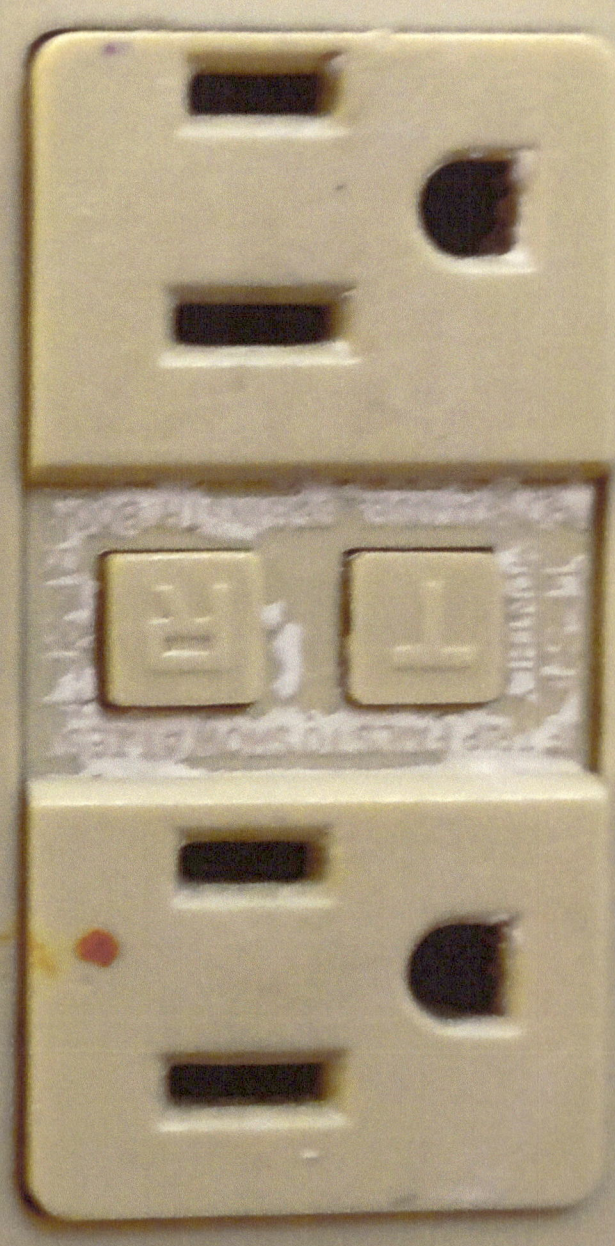

Sen was found in San Jose, USA,
disguised as a light sensor.

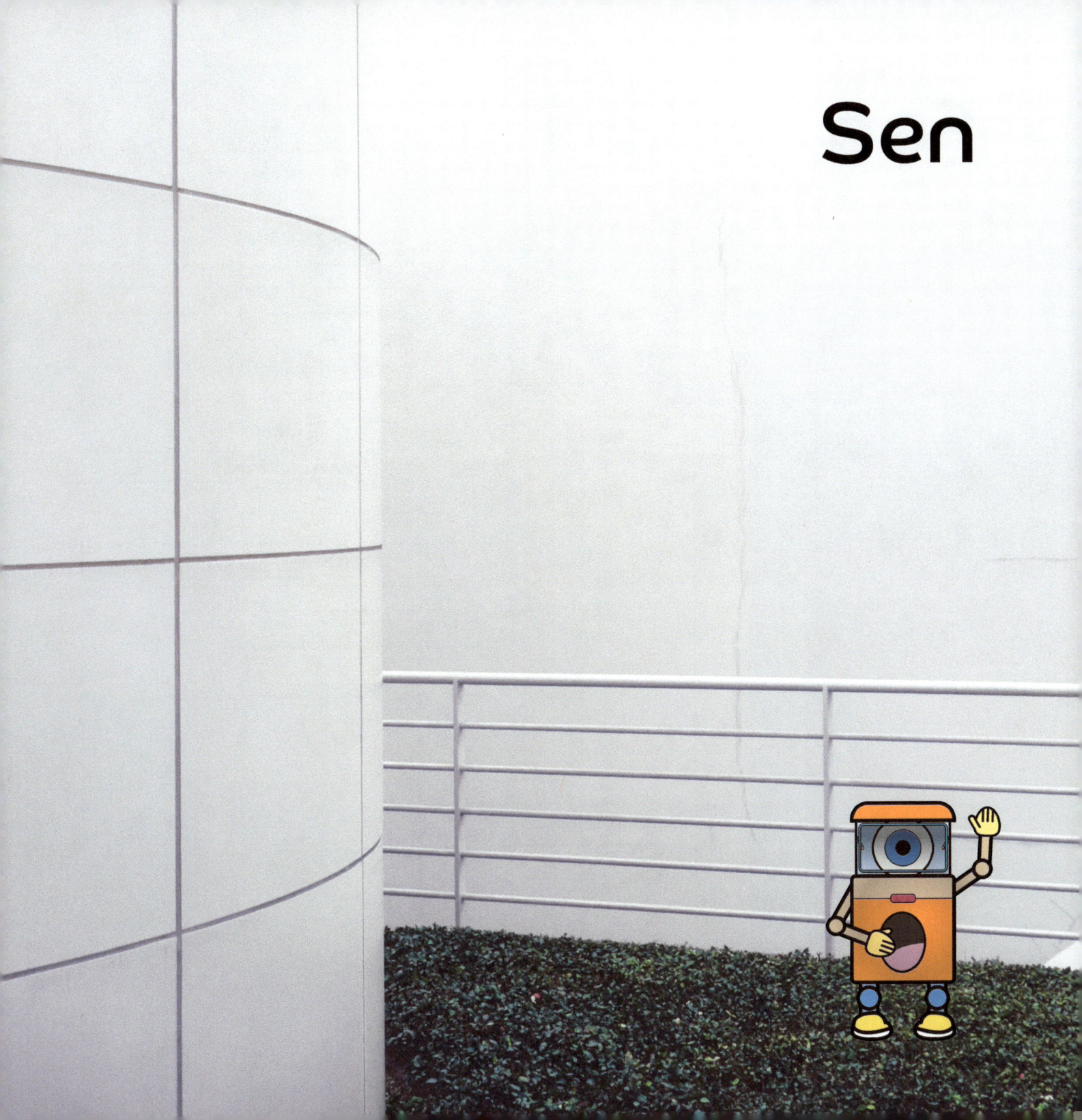

Sen

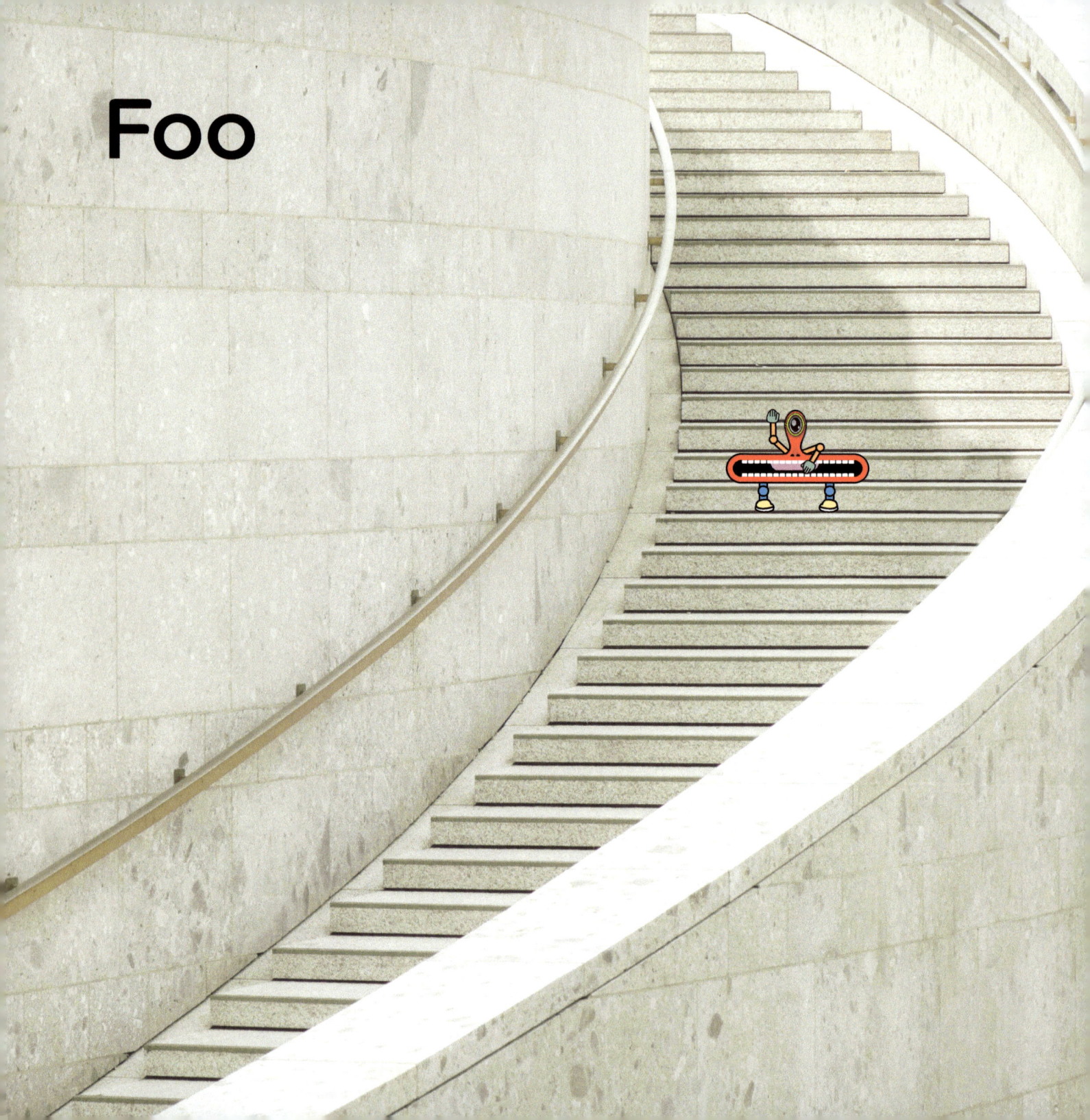

Foo

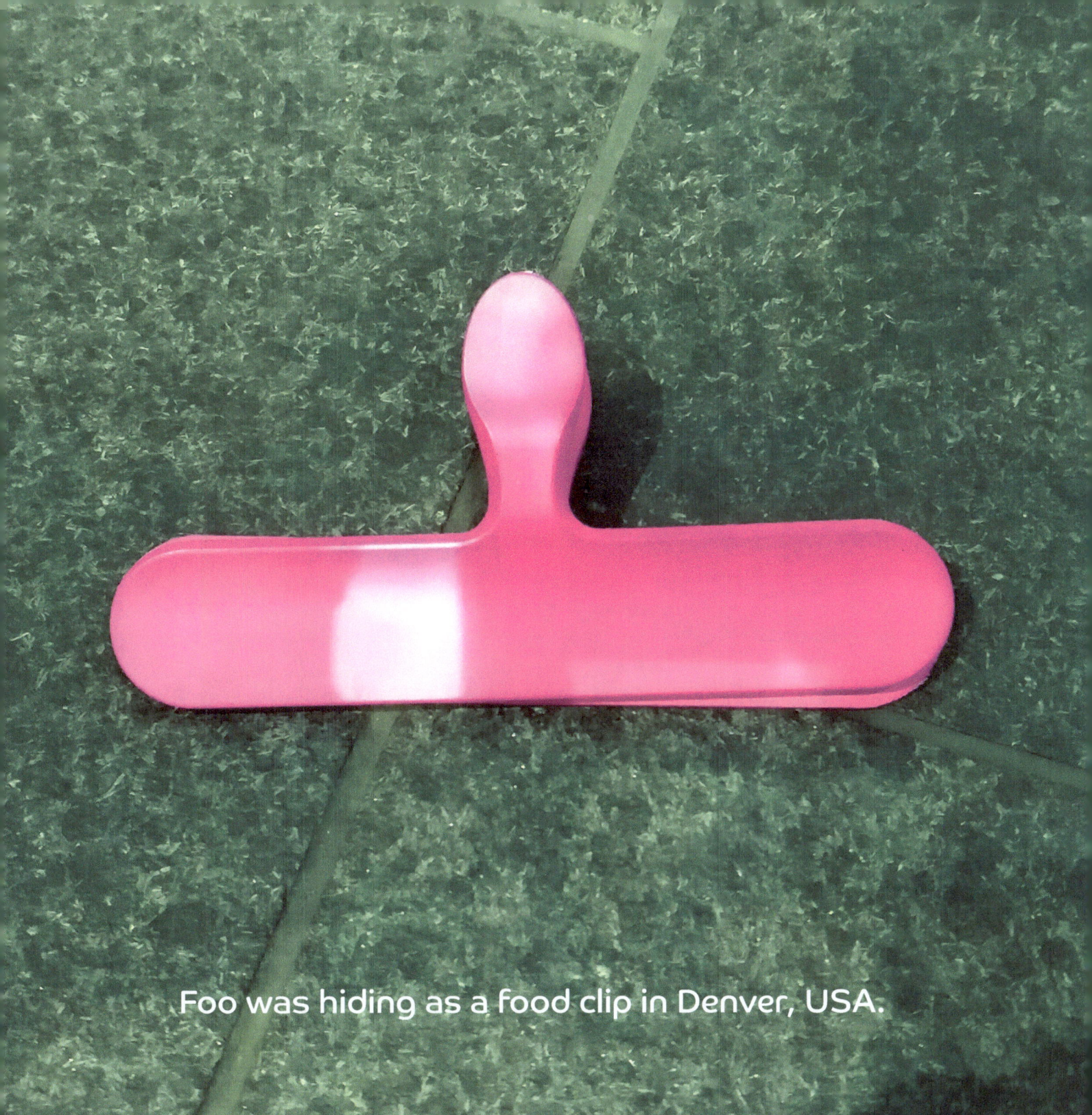

Foo was hiding as a food clip in Denver, USA.

In San Jose, USA, Loc was
camouflaged as a hotel door lock.

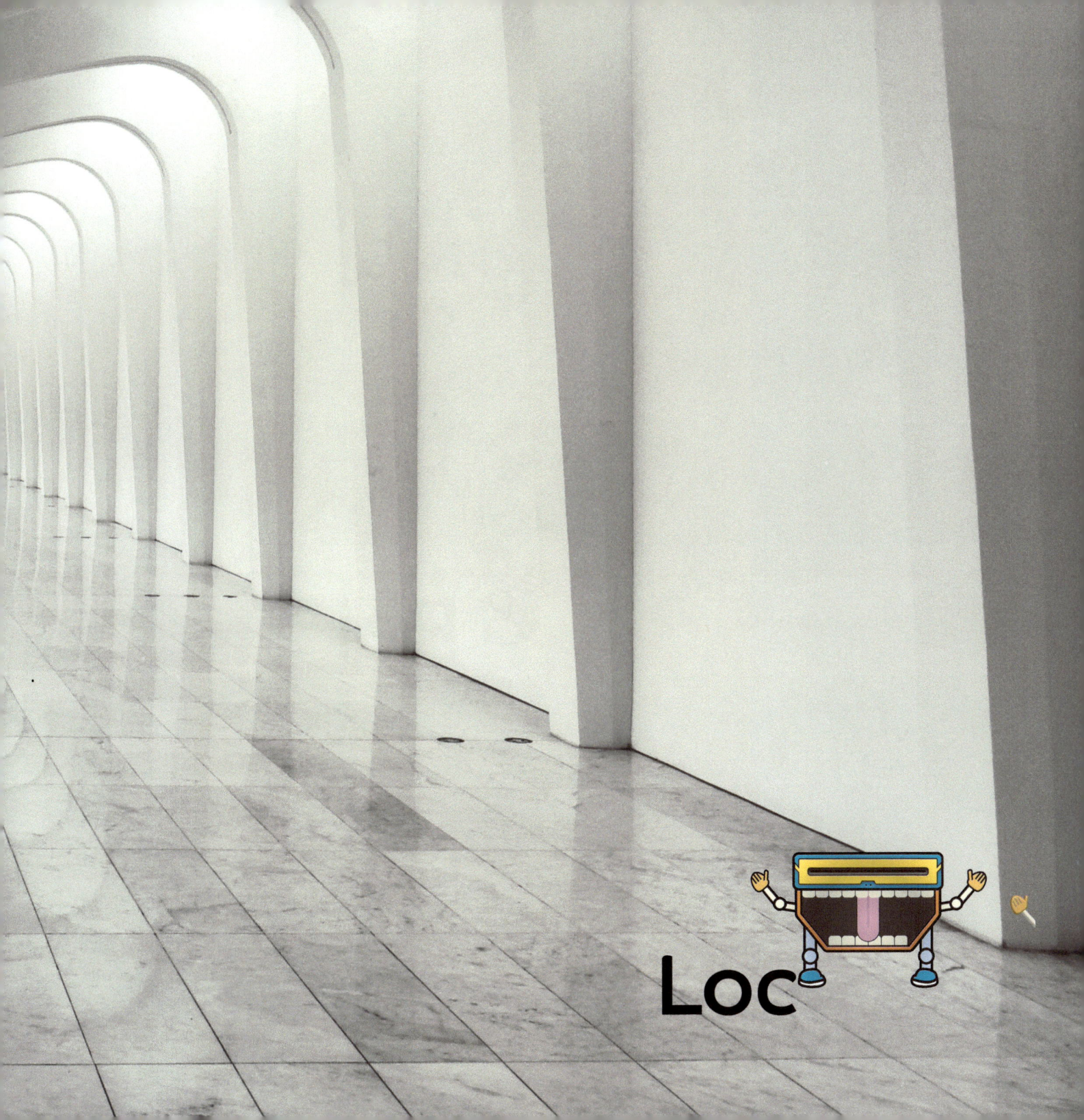

Loc

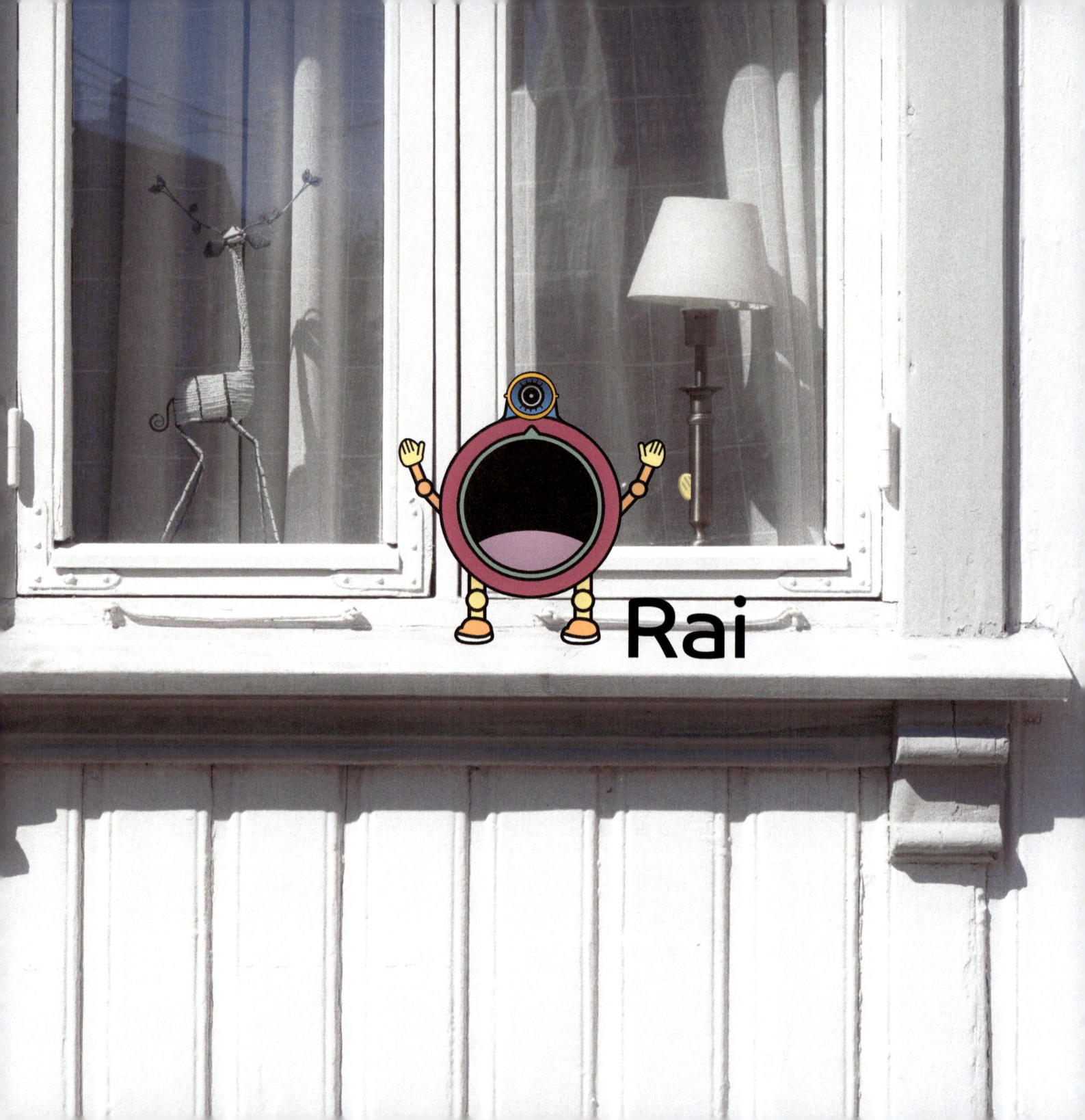

Rai

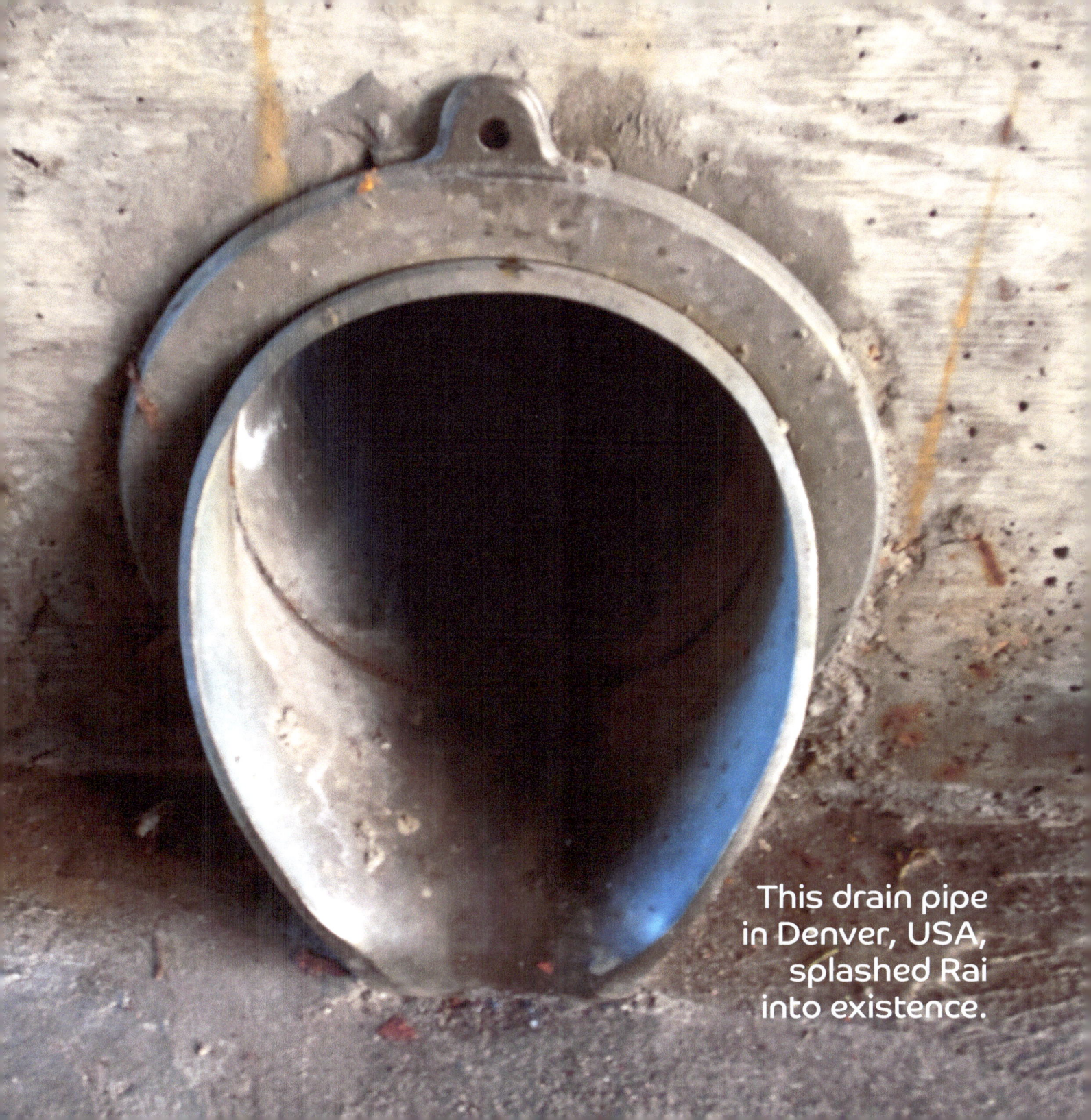

This drain pipe
in Denver, USA,
splashed Rai
into existence.

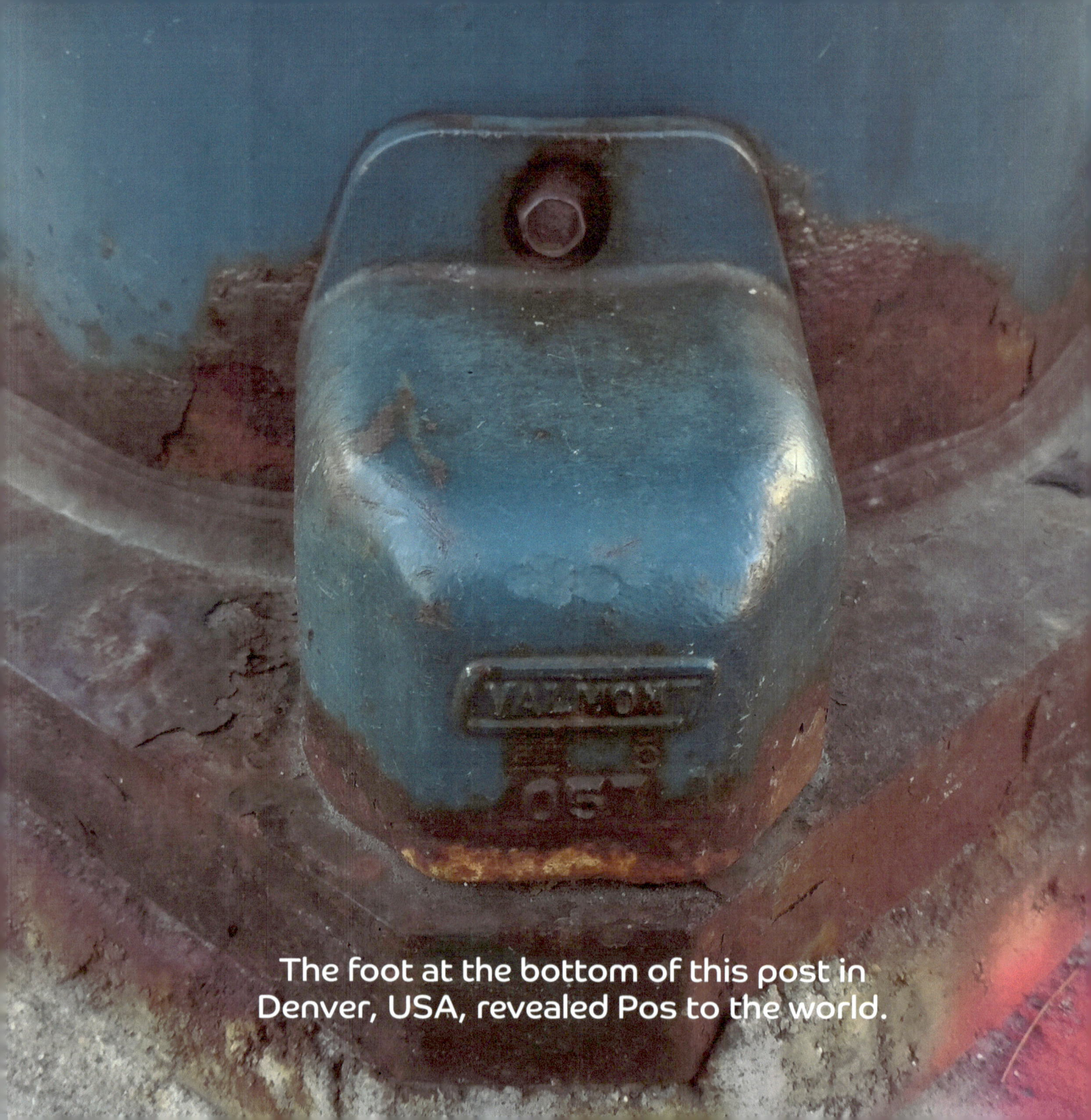

The foot at the bottom of this post in Denver, USA, revealed Pos to the world.

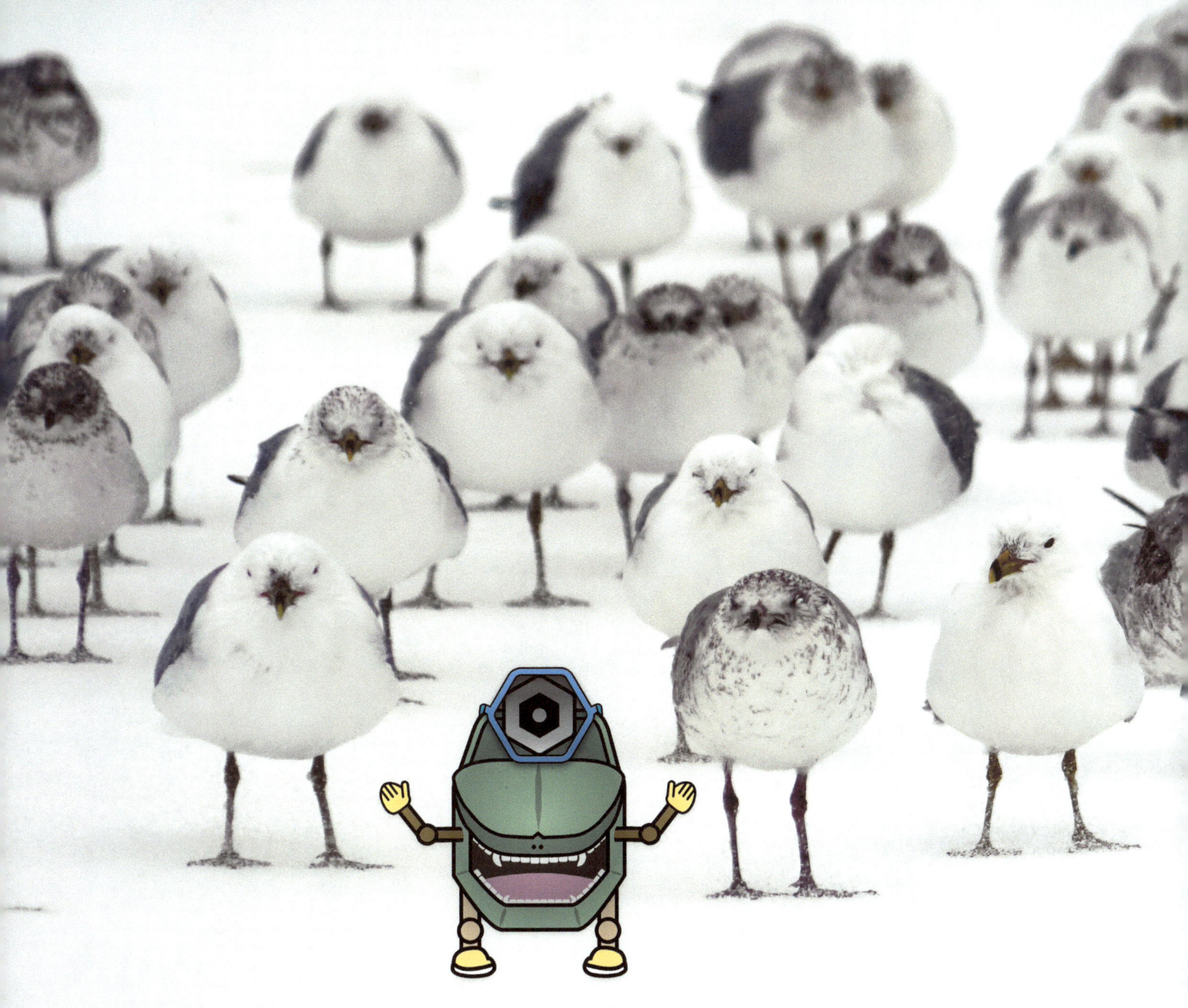

Pos

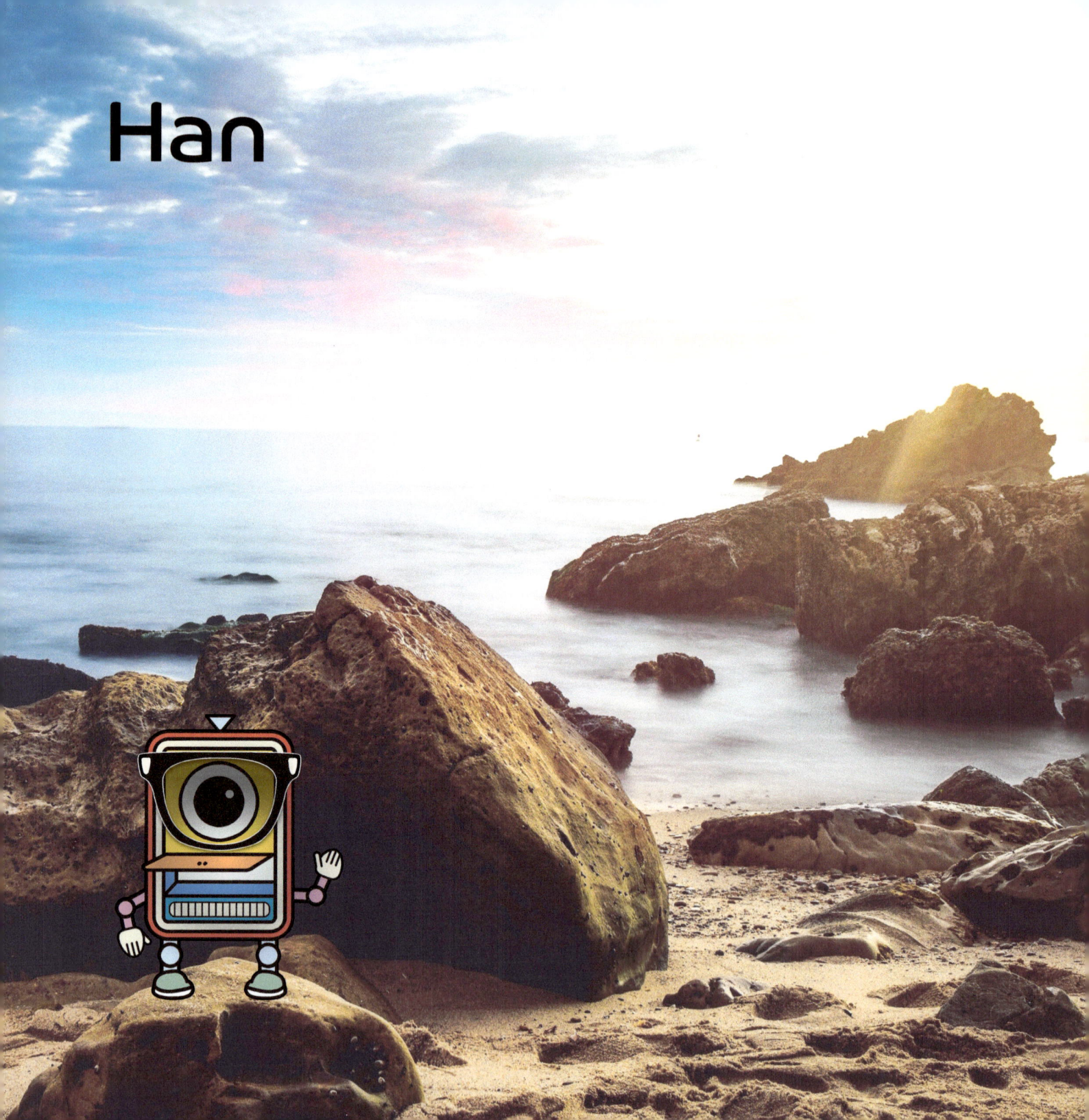

Han

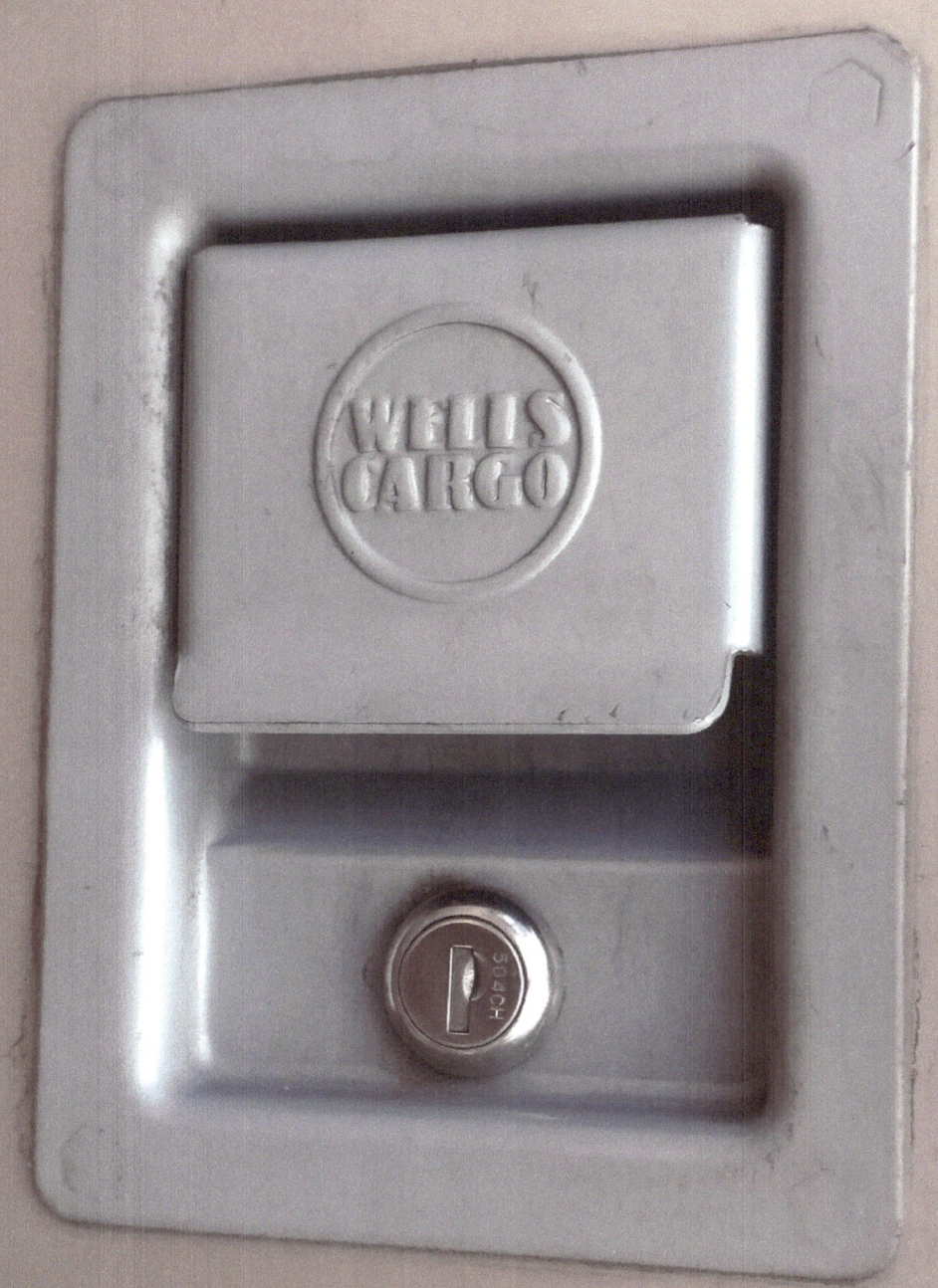

On the side of a horse box in Boulder, USA, this handle opened our consciousness to the existence of Han.

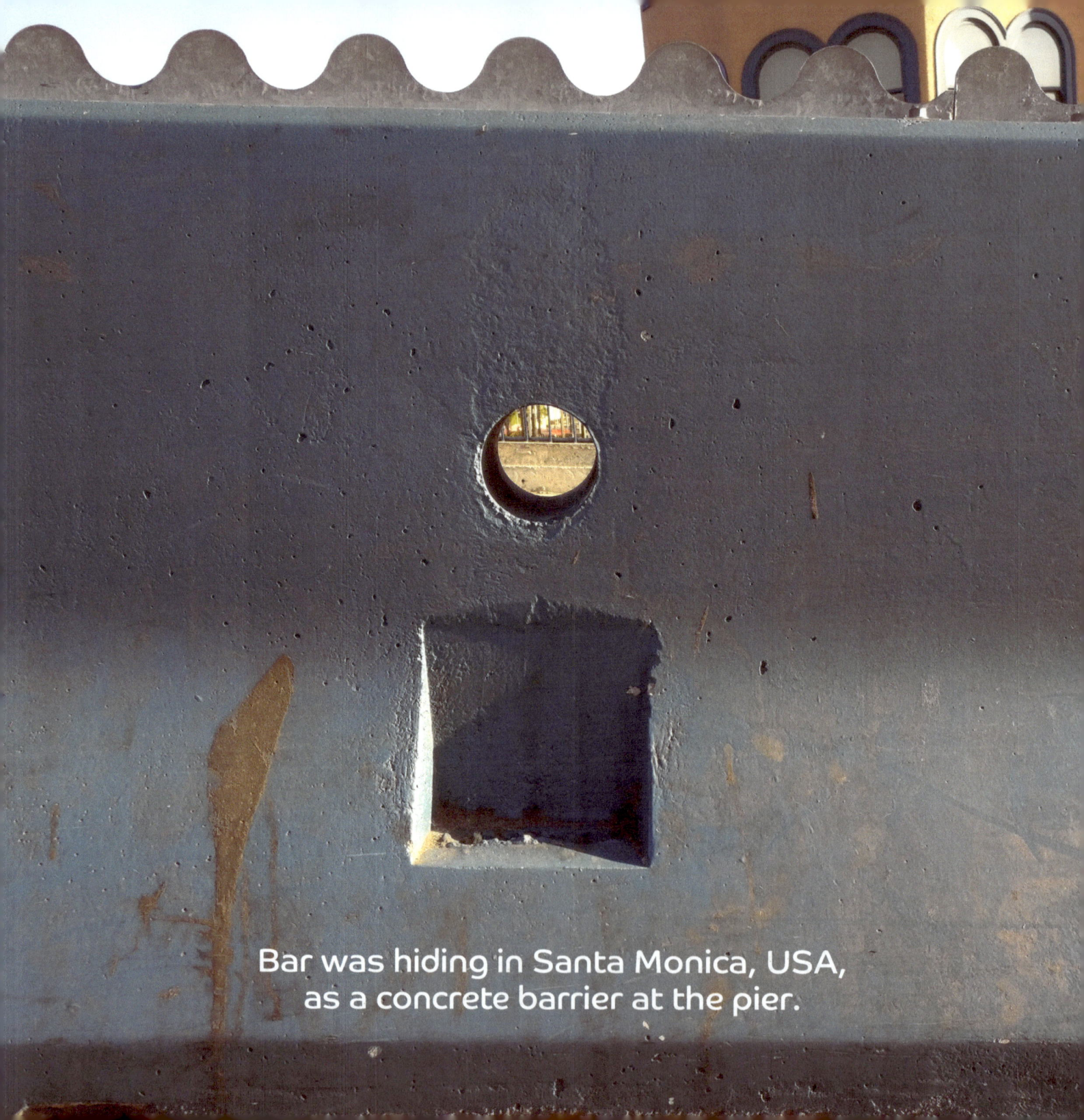

Bar was hiding in Santa Monica, USA,
as a concrete barrier at the pier.

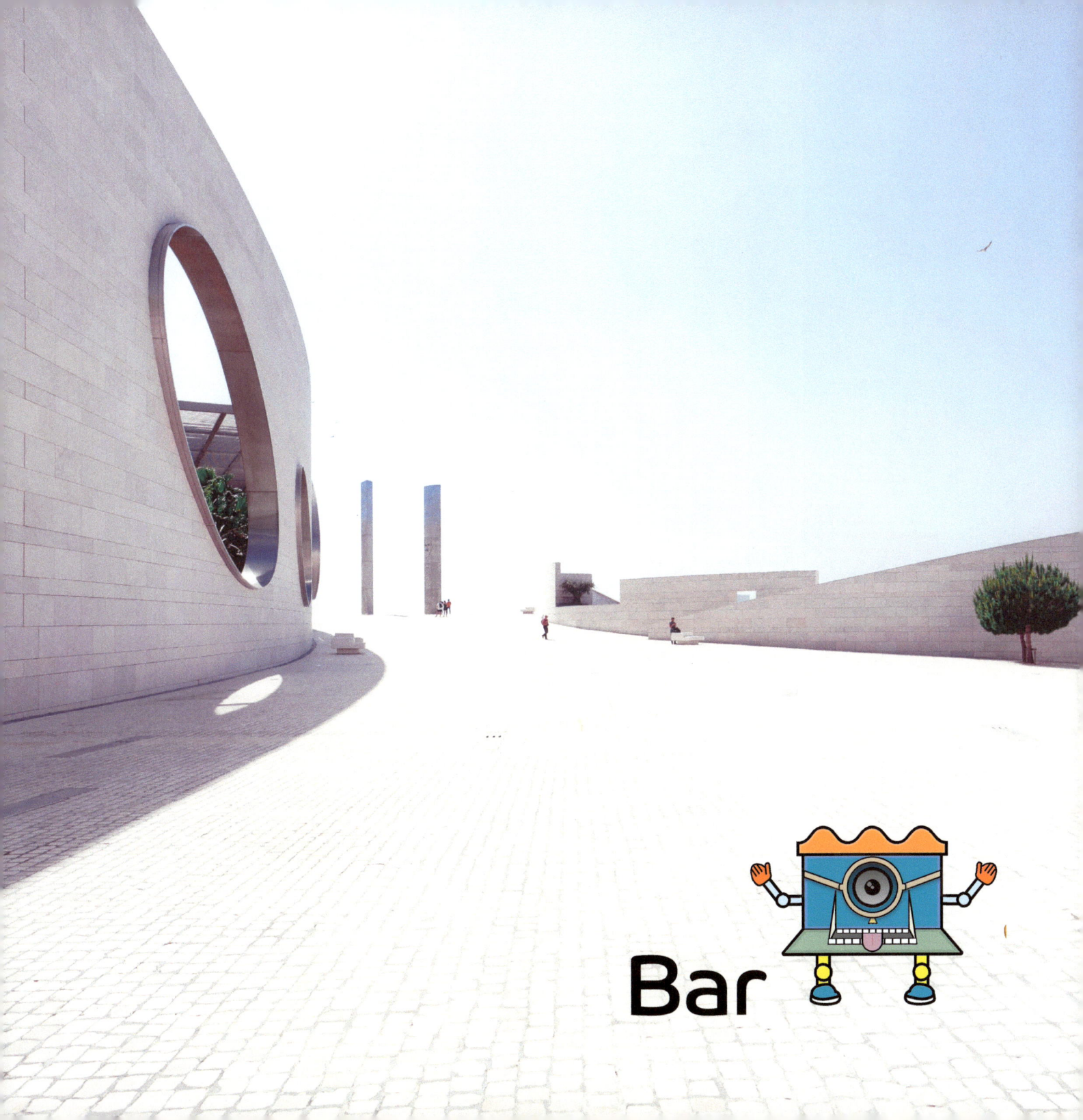

Bar

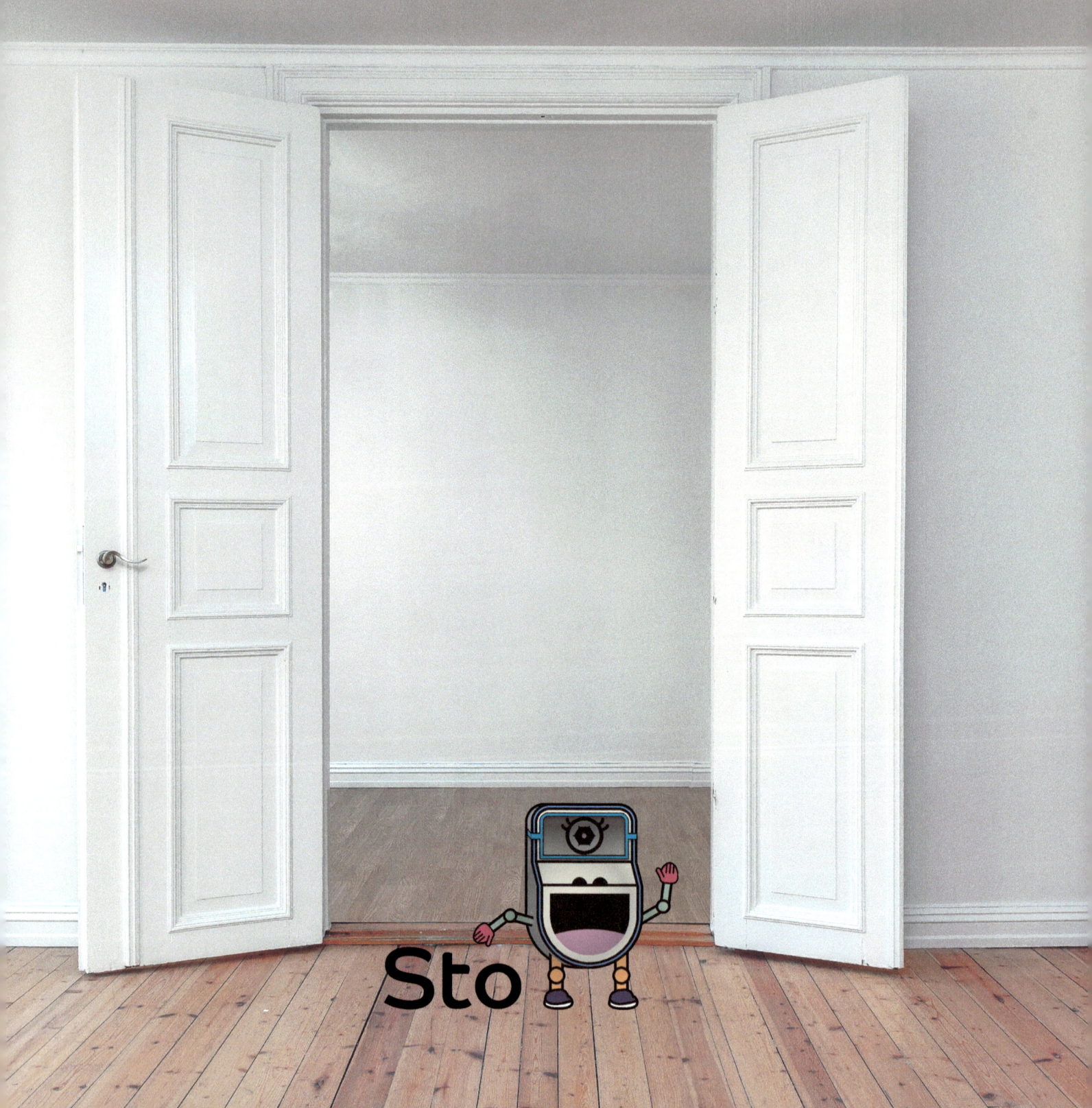

Sto

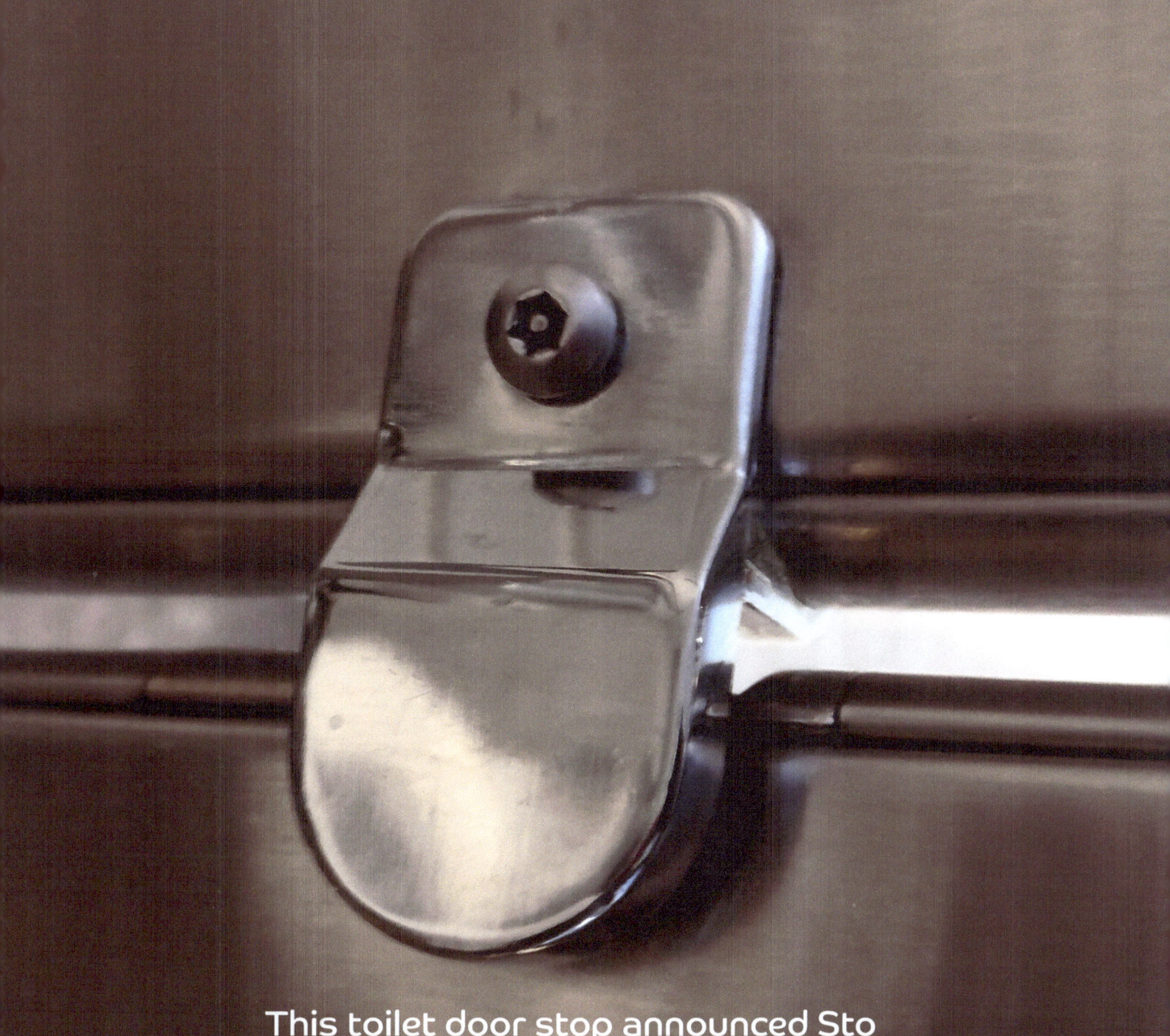

This toilet door stop announced Sto
to the universe in Chicago, USA.

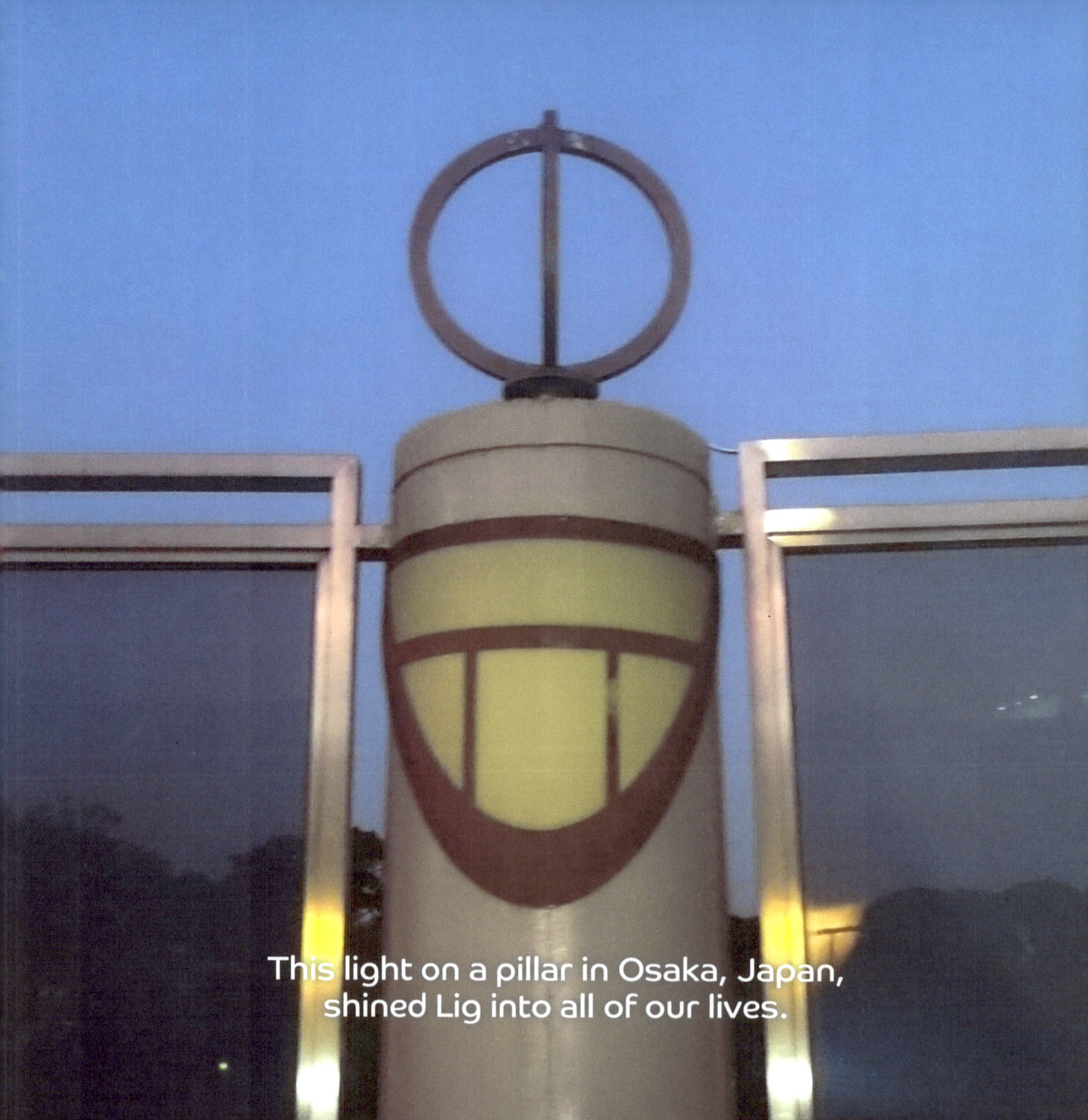

This light on a pillar in Osaka, Japan, shined Lig into all of our lives.

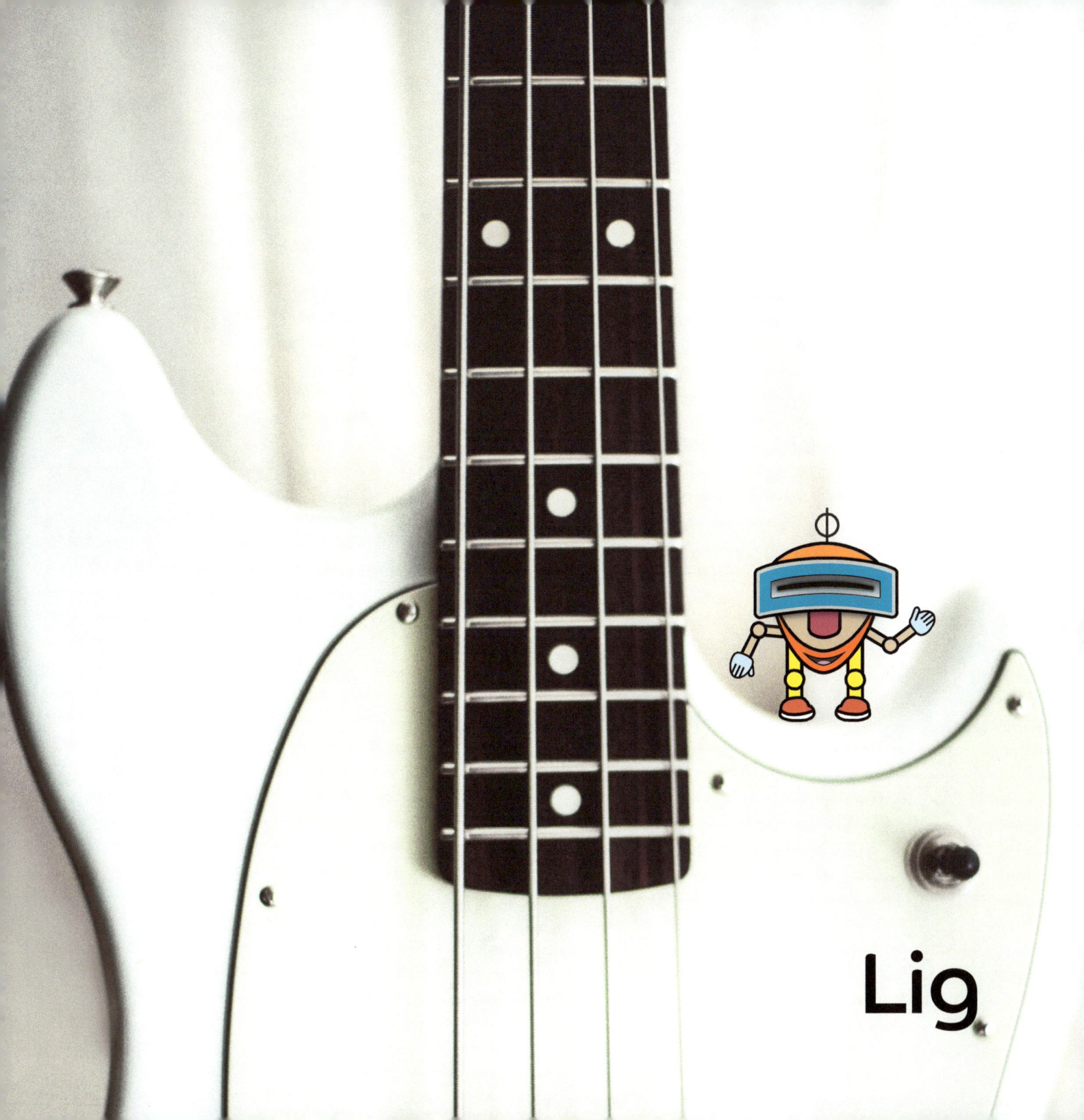

Lig

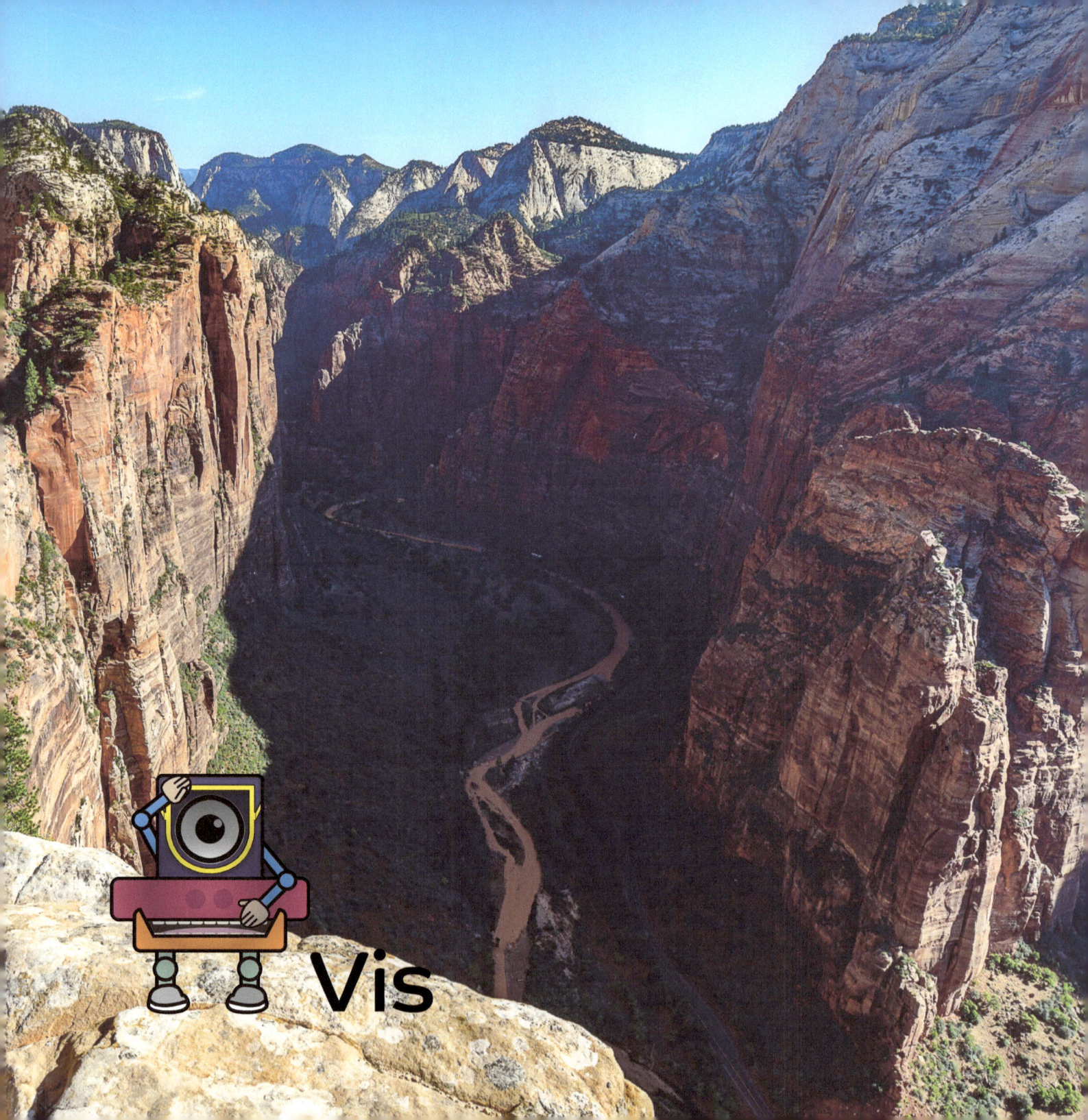

Vis

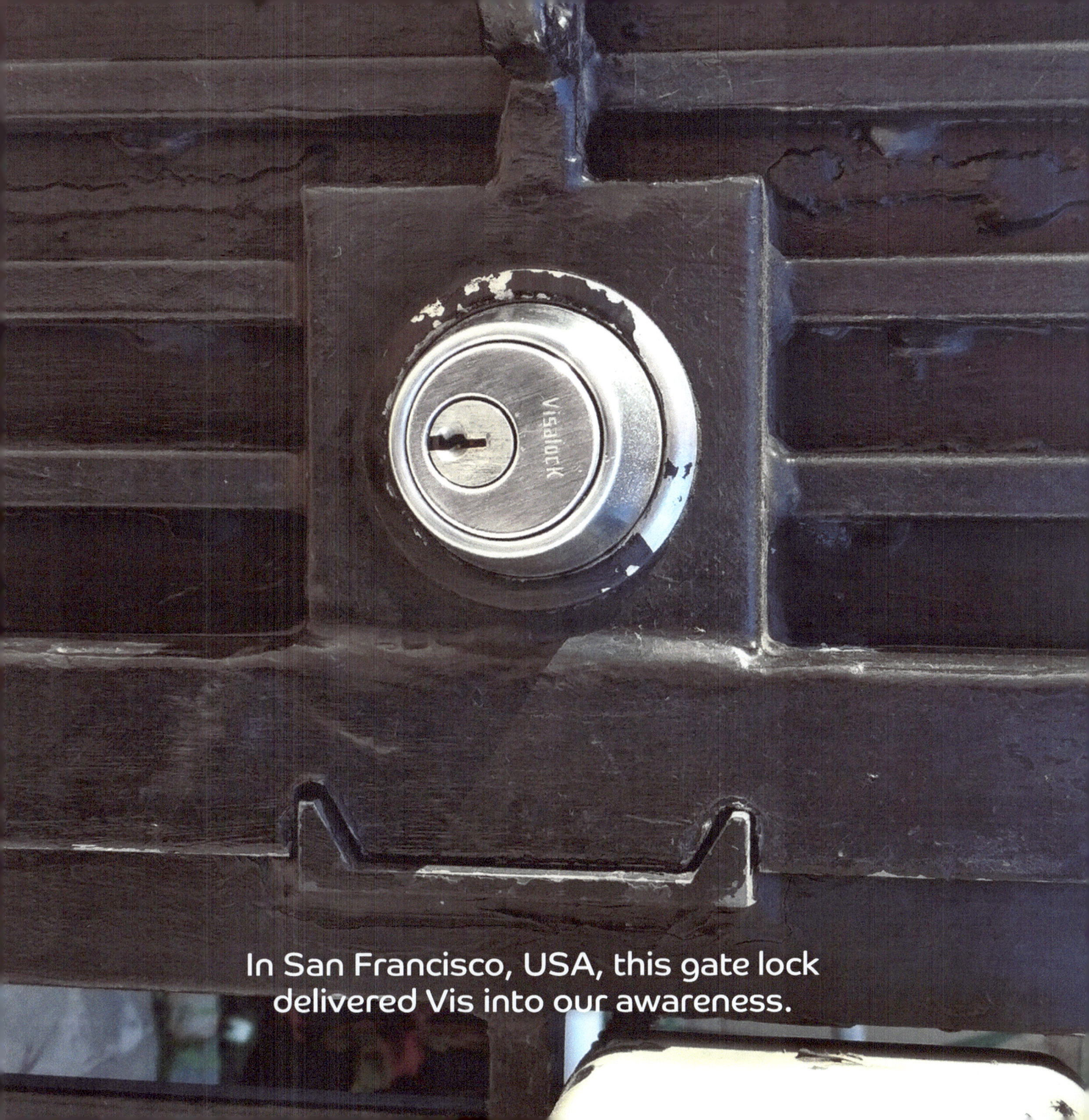

In San Francisco, USA, this gate lock delivered Vis into our awareness.

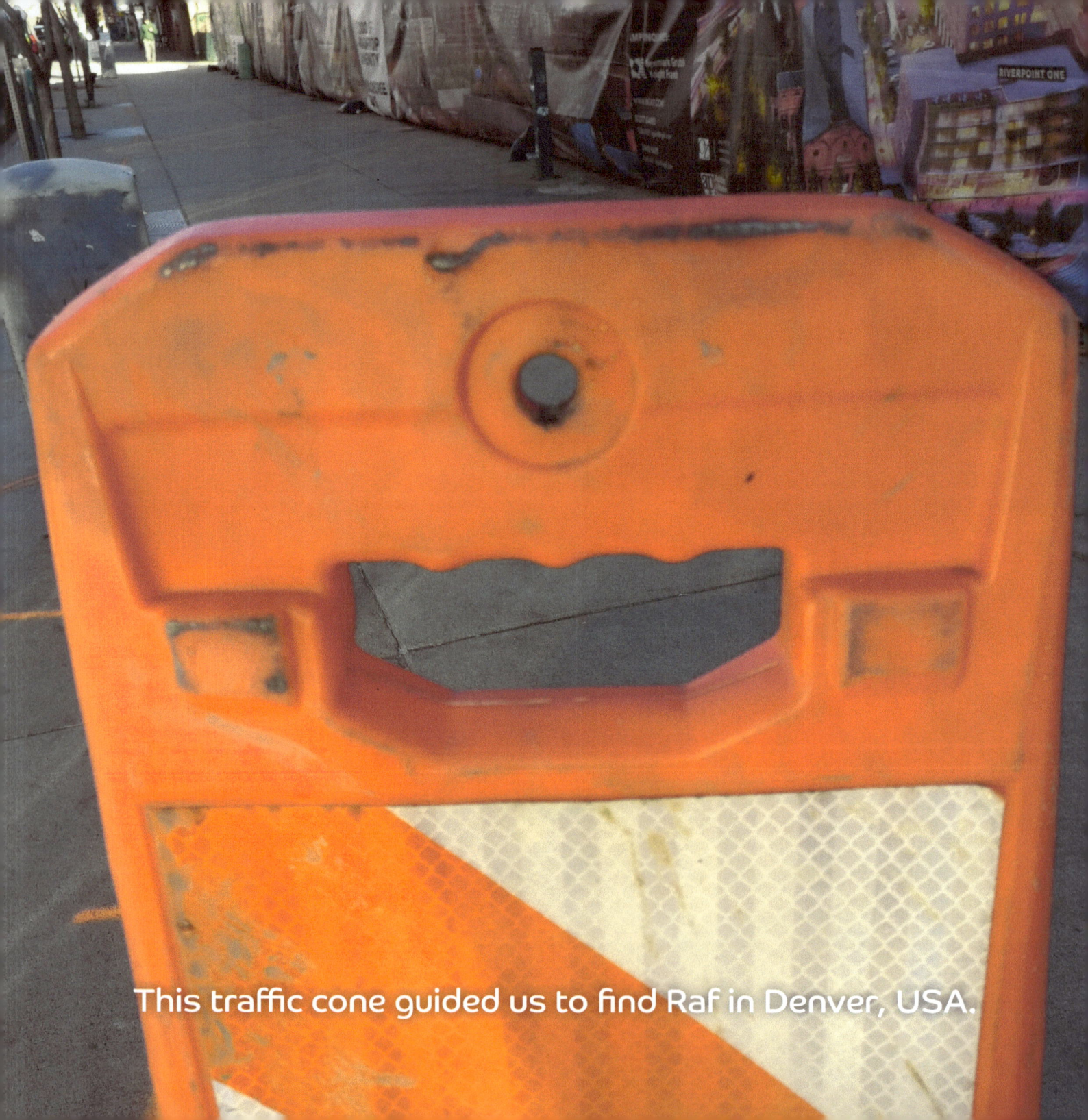

This traffic cone guided us to find Raf in Denver, USA.

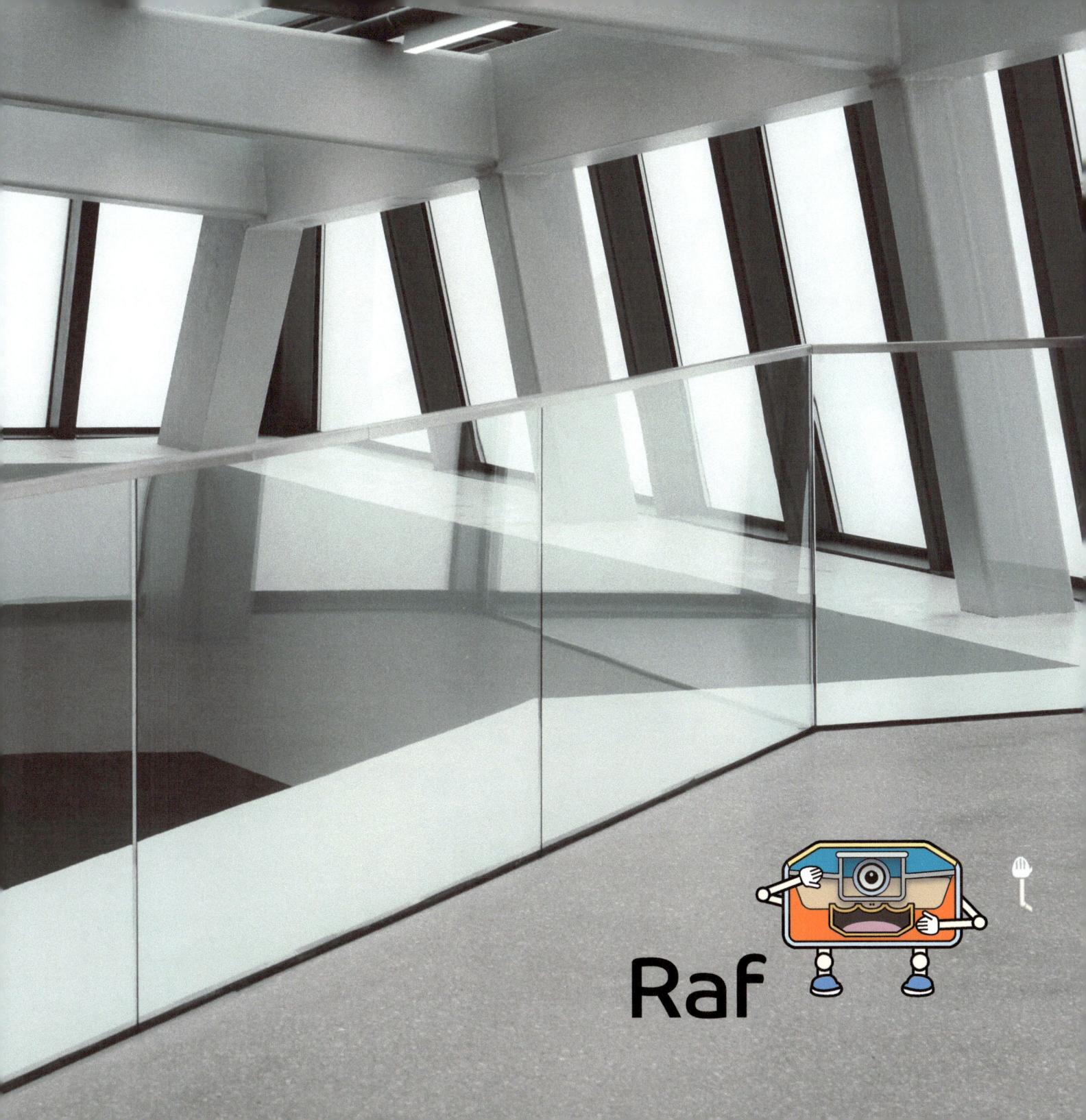

Raf

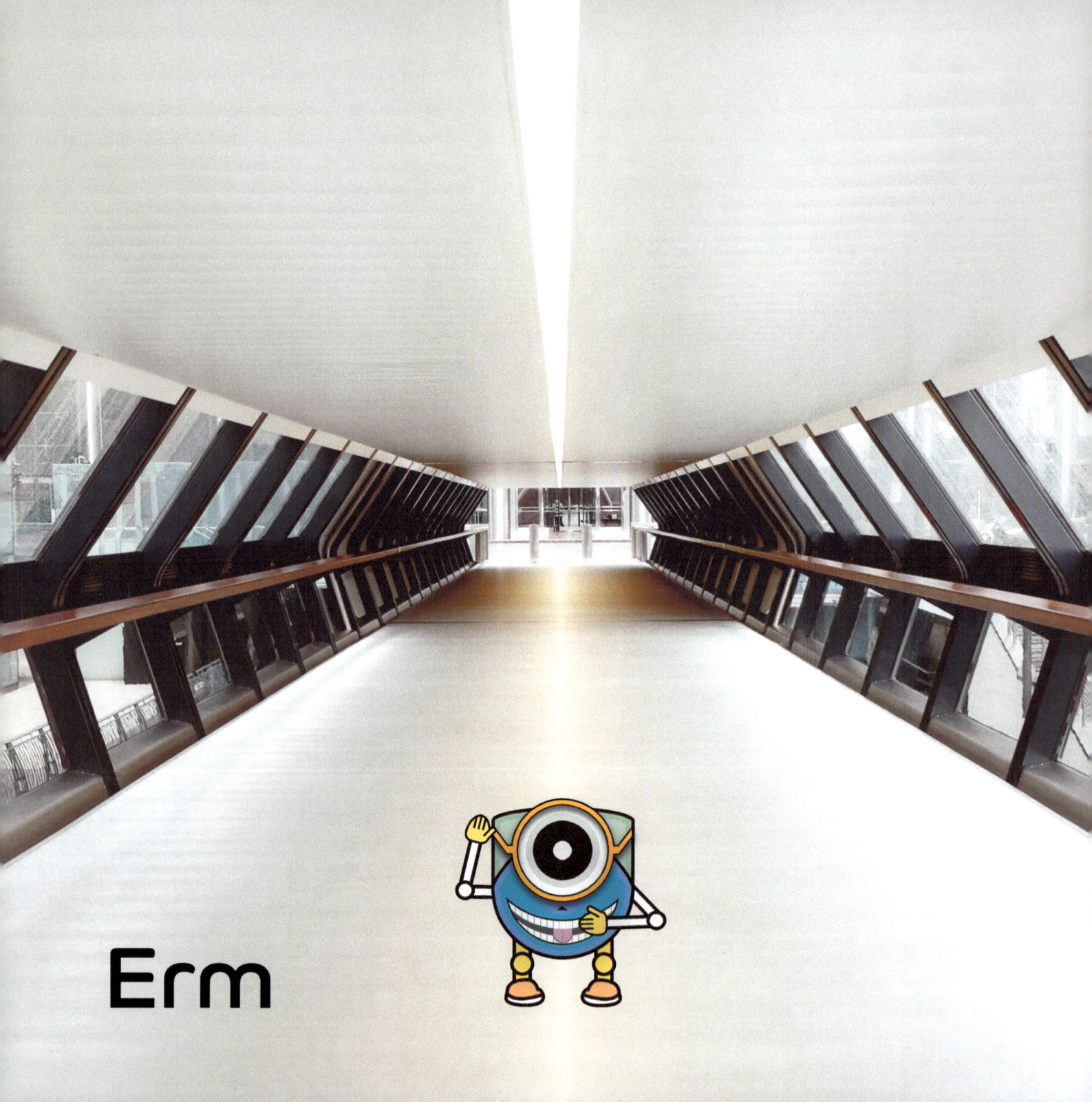

Erm

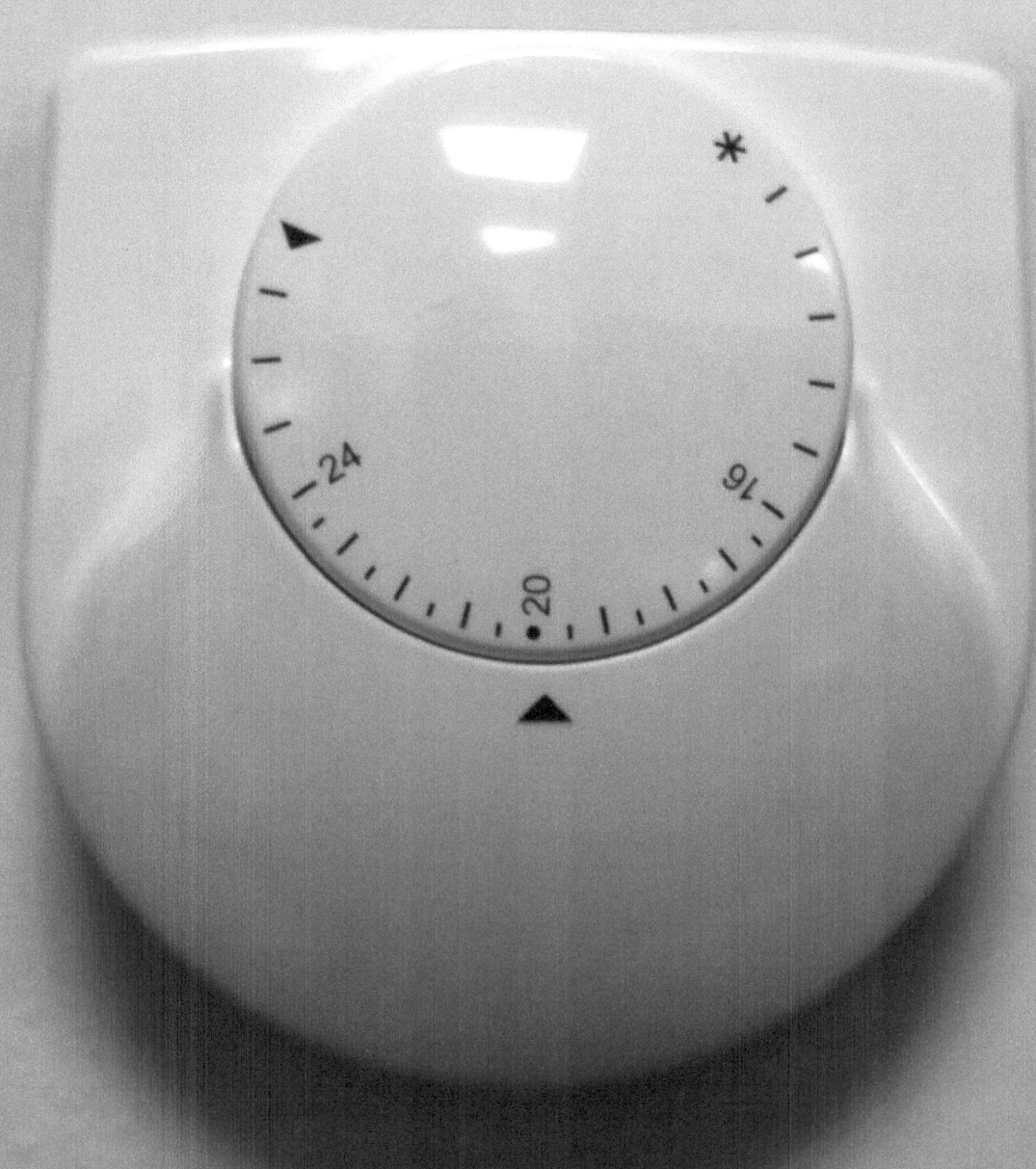

This thermostat warmed our hearts by revealing Erm to us all in Frome, UK.

CYCLOPED!

This book and the supporting website is a fictional story invented by myself to share the work I have created as a graphic artist.

I hope you enjoyed this book as much as I did creating it.

Best wishes,

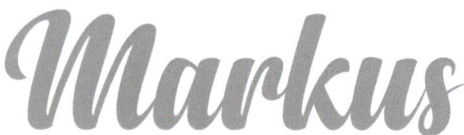

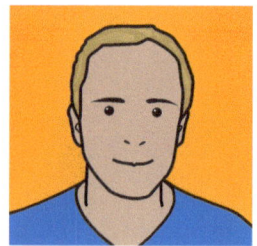

www.siklopp.com

MORE BOOKS BY R&Q

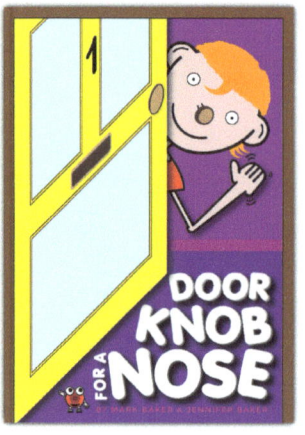

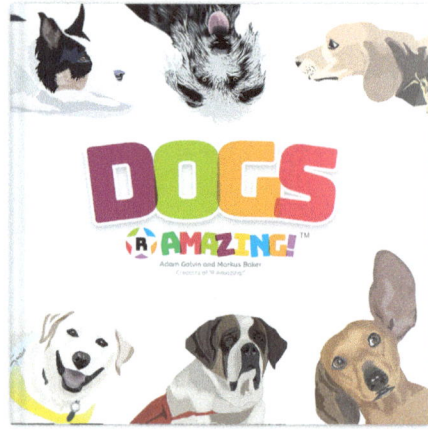

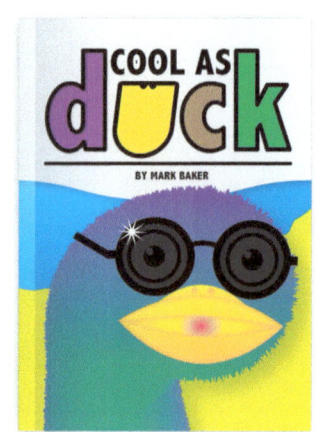

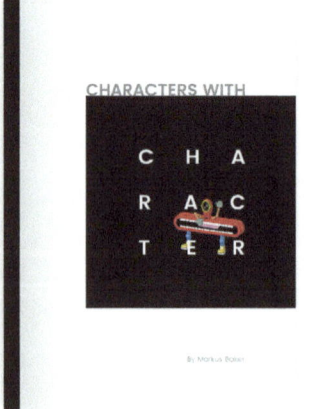

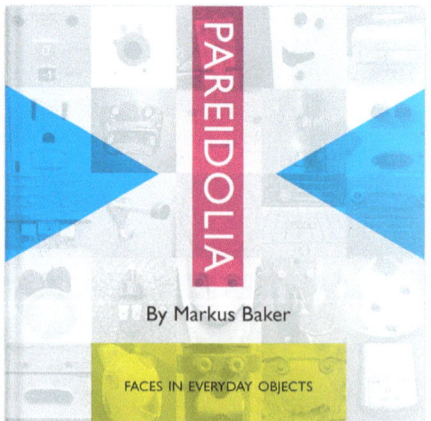

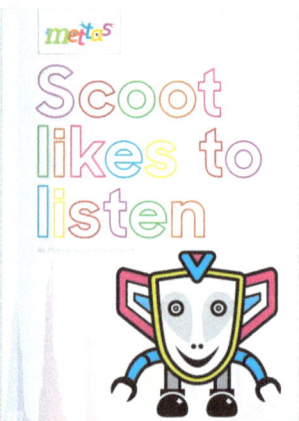